"The public response to my experiences as a Guantánamo prosecutor indicates that the moral and ethical treatment of detainees is an idea that resonates with Americans from across the spectrum of political and religious ideology. Our nation needs to lay claim to the humane treatment of detainees—not as Republicans or Democrats, but as Americans who recognize the inherent worth and value of fellow human beings, regardless of the despicable criminal acts they may have committed. Until now, the legal debate over detainee treatment has centered on what we *can* do with respect to permissible interrogation techniques. Lt. Col. Porter Harlow's excellent work adds an equally vigorous moral debate about what we *should* do as law-abiding Americans and human beings. Humane treatment of inhumane people is not a novel concept for people in the military, as exemplified by Harlow's keen insight and impeccable scholarship. His book is a welcome resource to all Americans now engaged in a global war on terrorism; it provides needed encouragement that our enemies will lose this war because we are better than they are, not because we are more inhumane."
—**V. Stuart Couch**, Lieutenant Colonel, U.S. Marine Corps (Retired)

"A worldview based on Scripture should be comprehensive and able to address even the hardest of ethical issues. Harlow has done just that and brings a sharp and analytical legal and theological perspective to a difficult and contested topic. Offering a biblical critique of enhanced interrogation techniques and working within the centuries-old framework of the just-war tradition, he shows that hard questions can be answered and that in a world of gray, black and white does exist."
—**Timothy J. Demy**, Professor of Military Ethics, U.S. Naval War College

"The recent history of the church in the United States, and of American Christian missions around the world, has been complicated by a series of major moral problems, including appropriate responses to

terrorism and potential terrorists. As a theologian, lawyer, and marine, Porter Harlow asks—and answers—ethical questions about methods of interrogation. What he has to say is thoughtful, respectful, and biblically responsible. I hope that not only Christian leaders but also politicians and practitioners will make the time to read this book."
—**Chad Van Dixhoorn**, Chancellor's Professor of Historical Theology, Reformed Theological Seminary, Washington, DC

"Porter Harlow has written a richly informed, morally compelling treatise on one of the signal ethical issues of our day. The treatment of the weak and the outcast is a sure test of a nation's character—and who has less status than a prisoner of war? Writing as a military officer, Harlow brings an insider's perspective to an abiding ethical question."
—**Daniel M. Doriani**, Vice President of Strategic Academic Initiatives and Professor of Theology, Covenant Theological Seminary

"There is nothing out there like Porter Harlow's study of interrogation techniques in the light of just-war theory. Learned, well informed, and, most importantly, profoundly biblical, this book should be read by every military authority, as well as by ordinary citizens who may not have carefully thought through the issues. At a moment when there is serious doubt about American foreign policy and about the role of armed intervention, the book will restore the hope that America can still find its way, if only it commits to principle and not to opportunism."
—**William Edgar**, Professor of Apologetics, Westminster Theological Seminary

"It is an honor to recommend this book. Terrorism roils the globe. Concern for security and safety cuts across ideological boundaries. But what should be the Christian approach to our government's treatment of terrorists? As a former U.S. Marine officer and military lawyer, Porter Harlow has seen military legal culture from the inside. As a

Christian theologian, he offers biblical and theological analysis and critique of the treatment of prisoners. He challenges evangelical political assumptions and, like John Calvin before him, urges that public life must reflect the righteousness of the sovereign God. In this polarized moment, Christians cannot afford to ignore his call to honor the image of God in all."
—**Howard Griffith**, Associate Professor of Systematic Theology and Academic Dean, Reformed Theological Seminary, Washington, DC

"Lieutenant Colonel J. Porter Harlow is one of the best people to write this book. He is a seminary graduate who is also a Marine officer and an attorney. Porter leads us on a clear investigation of how to think theologically about the torture and mistreatment of detainees. Torture is a violation of the image of God in humanity. This book explores whether some of the U.S. methods of interrogating detainees have violated biblical requirements and just-war standards that reflect those requirements."
—**Justin S. Holcomb**, Episcopal Priest; Professor of Theology, Reformed Theological Seminary and Gordon-Conwell Theological Seminary

"Porter Harlow's book is profound and deeply disturbing. It is profound yet clear, forceful yet graceful, rooted in ancient wisdom yet contemporary. It is deeply disturbing in its accounts of the vicious and dehumanizing torture of fellow human beings, however evil those men may have been. But it is perhaps even more disturbing in its display of how easily and even ridiculously certain 'evangelical' theologians twist Scripture and reason, and discard centuries of carefully established just-war tradition, bringing shame on the church and putting the bodies and souls of United States military personnel in peril.

"Without any exaggeration, war is deadly serious. Any degree of sophistry or casuistry from those who enter into it, but especially from

those who would establish or defend policies that direct the waging of it, brings horrific consequences. Porter Harlow argues that 'the minds and hearts of evangelical political leaders, military service members, seminary professors, pastors, and church members were not prepared to recognize and honor the *imago Dei* in the detainees captured during the global war on terrorism.' He also argues that by dishonoring, shaming, or attacking the image of God in the prisoner, we who are Christians dishonor, shame, and attack the image of Christ in ourselves. We become less human and less Christian."
—**Jeffrey D. Hutchinson**, Assistant Minister, Christ Presbyterian Church, New Haven, CT; former Surface Warfare Officer, U.S. Navy

"Following 9/11, the United States used an 'end-justifies-the-means' logic to sideline historical prohibitions on waterboarding, physical violence in interrogations, and the dehumanization of detainees. The slippery slope of moral relativism was illuminated during this period, and it remains a dangerous influence in our national security decision-making process today. Porter Harlow's work is extraordinarily important in highlighting this danger, and explains with nuanced sophistication how realism can allow for almost anything to be done in the name of 'military necessity.' For those who believe that our national leaders must demonstrate the moral courage expounded by the just-war traditions of Augustine, Aquinas, Calvin, Murray, and Ramsey, Porter Harlow's book is essential reading."
—**Shane R. Reeves**, Lieutenant Colonel, U.S. Army; Professor and Deputy Head, Department of Law, United States Military Academy, West Point, NY

"Think that the only people opposed to the use of torture against terrorists are liberals and/or antimilitary? Think again. Actually, those who led our country into the moral gutter of 'enhanced interrogation techniques' were the ones who turned their backs on conservative legal and theological traditions, and very often tended not to have significant military experience personally. Reflecting historic Reformed orthodoxy, no less than the consensus of the professional officer corps, Marine Lt. Col. Harlow has written the definitive legal and theological refutation of these sub-Christian practices. As the nation decides on its next commander-in-chief, this excellent book is not to be missed."

—**William M. Schweitzer**, PCA Missionary; Professor of Systematic Theology, Greenville Presbyterian Theological Seminary (UK campus); former Captain, U.S. Marine Corps; served in Operations Enduring Freedom, Iraqi Freedom, and Southern Watch

"Christians watch the news with heavy (and sometimes angry) hearts as terrorists continue to massacre human lives without remorse. Unfortunately, terrorist activity often produces a vacuum of compassion for terrorists themselves. We conveniently forget that every act of terrorism against humanity pales in comparison to humanity's terrorism against God. We do well to remember that the apostle Paul terrorized the church before the grace of Jesus Christ seized hold of him. My conscience, for one, is far too easily desensitized to the realities that detained terrorists are made in the image of God, are not beyond the grace of God, and should be afforded humane treatment by the people of God. This timely book dealt a sorely needed prick to my calloused conscience.

"Terrorism has a shelf life; it will not last forever. God's Word, however, will never pass away. Though surprising to some, Scripture does have something to say about the role of torture, and it is a message that the church needs to hear. I have every confidence that this tightly reasoned, Scripture-laden book will prove helpful to the church as she endeavors to live *Coram Deo*, even in times of war."

—**Joe Steele**, Pastor, Woodland Presbyterian Church (PCA); former U.S. Marine Corps F-18 pilot; flew combat missions in Operation Iraqi Freedom

"Porter Harlow has given us a clear and engaging appeal to think biblically about detainee treatment in war. His analysis is brief but surprisingly thorough, and Christians need to read it and pray over it before they blindly affirm views that call for a 'harder line' or a recovery of torture methods that would 'defend America's honor.' There is much to ponder on the issue of how we treat our enemies, and Harlow has given us a wonderful analysis of both the biblical evidence and the theological arguments for and against his views so that we can form our own opinions. This is just the kind of analysis that we urge on our students in Study Centers work, and I recommend it highly."
—**Andrew H. Trotter Jr.**, Executive Director, Consortium of Christian Study Centers

"In this timely book, Colonel Harlow marshals the witness of Scripture and the wisdom of Christian tradition against the temptation to fear-driven expediency. May the church heed—and take up—his clarion call to faithfulness in the conduct of war."
—**William N. Wilder**, Executive Director, Center for Christian Study, Charlottesville, VA

How Should We Treat Detainees?

Reformed Academic Dissertations

A Series

Series Editor

John J. Hughes

How Should We Treat Detainees?

An Examination of "Enhanced Interrogation Techniques" under the Light of Scripture and the Just War Tradition

J. Porter Harlow, M.A.R., J.D., LL.M.

P&R PUBLISHING
P.O. BOX 817 • PHILLIPSBURG • NEW JERSEY 08865-0817

How Should We Treat Detainees? An Examination of Enhanced Interrogation Techniques under the Light of Scripture and the Just War Tradition. J. Porter Harlow, M.A.R., J.D., LL.M. Submitted to Reformed Theological Seminary, Washington, DC., 2014, for the M.A.R. degree. Supervisor: Howard Griffith.

Italics within Scripture quotations indicate emphasis added.

ISBN: 978-1-62995-288-8 (pbk)
ISBN: 978-1-62995-289-5 (ePub)
ISBN: 978-1-62995-290-1 (Mobi)

Printed in the United States of America

This book is dedicated to

My wife, Cathy,

Our three children, Andrew, Grace, and Calvin,

And the many U.S. service members who have served our country,

Especially those who have served in Afghanistan and Iraq since the terrorist attacks on the United States on September 11th, 2001.

O may thy soldiers, faithful, true, and bold,
fight as the saints who nobly fought of old,
and win with them the victor's crown of gold.
Alleluia! Alleluia!

The golden evening brightens in the west,
soon, soon to faithful warriors comes their rest;
sweet is the calm of paradise the blest.
Alleluia! Alleluia!

But lo! there breaks a yet more glorious day;
the saints triumphant rise in bright array;
the King of glory passes on his way.
Alleluia! Alleluia!

From earth's wide bounds, from ocean's farthest coast,
through gates of pearl stream in the countless host,
singing to Father, Son and Holy Ghost.
Alleluia! Alleluia!

"*For All the Saints*" by William Walsham How

Contents

Series Introduction

P&R Publishing has a long and distinguished history of publishing carefully selected, high-value theological books in the Reformed tradition. Many theological books begin as dissertations, but many dissertations are worthy of publication in their own right. Realizing this, P&R has launched the Reformed Academic Dissertation (RAD) program to publish top-tier dissertations (Ph.D., Th.D., D.Min., and Th.M.) that advance biblical and theological scholarship by making distinctive contributions in the areas of theology, ethics, biblical studies, apologetics, and counseling.

Dissertations in the RAD series are *curated*, which means that they are carefully selected, on the basis of strong recommendations by the authors' supervisors and examiners and by our internal readers, to be part of our collection. Each selected dissertation will provide clear, fresh, and engaging insights about significant theological issues.

A number of theological institutions have partnered with us to recommend dissertations that they believe worthy of publication in the RAD series. Not only does this provide increased visibility for participating institutions, it also makes outstanding dissertations available to a broad range of readers, while helping to introduce promising authors to the publishing world.

We look forward to seeing the RAD program grow into a large collection of curated dissertations that will help to advance Reformed scholarship and learning.

John J. Hughes
Series Editor

Foreword

Christians in America today live in a time when the spiritual heritage of our nation is rapidly collapsing. For most Bible-believers, this "culture war" consists of our moral and political struggle against abortion, sexual indecency, and the corruption of marriage. We see a frightening barbarism flowing from the halls of liberal political power and on the screens of an increasingly debased media establishment. Yet one of the most significant cultural watersheds of our time has nothing to do with the sexual revolution or progressive politicians. Quite to the contrary, this moral affront was established as national policy during the administration of a conservative, evangelical President—George W. Bush—and was approved and defended by none other than the Christian right wing. I refer to the moral crisis associated with the official endorsement of torture in the interrogation of military prisoners.

When I first learned that the Bush administration was employing the torture procedure known as *waterboarding*, my initial revulsion arose not from the Bible but from my childhood memories. I was born in 1960 to a military family. My grandfather was a highly decorated tank general who served with distinction under George S. Patton Jr. during World War II. My father was a tank colonel who spent two years of my childhood fighting in Vietnam. Growing up on Army bases, I accumulated poignant memories of the many military funerals I attended for the fathers of friends and neighbors. To this day, the playing of taps evokes deep feelings of sorrow in my heart. Another memory is of receiving a POW bracelet to wear when I was in the fourth grade. The year was 1969, and I was nine years old. Every day I bore the name of an American pilot who was languishing in prison—probably the Hanoi Hilton, I was told—and I offered daily prayers for his protection and help.

It was right about that time that news was coming back from the war of the torture of our captive men. I soon became acquainted with terms such as *the rope trick*—terms for the ways in which our fathers and sons were being subjected to terrible suffering to coerce them into betraying their country. Well do I remember the feeling that this information produced in my young heart: the feeling was hatred. I burned with moral indignation against the kind of men who would torture American prisoners. Our men were no longer combatants! They were no longer flying planes or dropping bombs! They were prisoners at the mercy of their captors! Day after day, I prayed that "my POW" would not be tortured. When my father returned to Vietnam in my sixth-grade year, I prayed that he would be protected from death, capture, and torture from our heinous enemy. Long after the war ended with the declaration of peace, the indignation inspired by the torture of our men barred actual feelings of reconciliation.

During and after the Vietnam War, the United States' moral opposition to officially sanctioned torture was absolute. As a young combat officer, I attended lectures given by such heroes as General Robbie Risner and Admiral James Stockdale, who recounted the terrors they survived in North Vietnamese camps and provided inspiring tales of how they maintained their dignity and sanity under torture. We were given copies of Risner's book *The Passing of the Night*, and read it with tears on our cheeks. In the Army's training schools, a good deal of the ethics instruction emphasized the moral abhorrence of torture and our strict duty as officers to take effective measures against it. Well do I remember speaking to my grandfather, Major General James Phillips, about this subject. "We must not descend to the moral level of our enemies," he insisted. "If in order to win a war we employ the evil practices of our enemies, we have in fact lost the war," he instructed me. Later in my military career, I passed on this ethic to the cadets at West Point, where I served as assistant professor. American soldiers are not brutes, we taught, but honorable defenders of human life and dignity. We did not teach the kind of situational ethics that says that our own survival justifies any behavior. We admitted, of course, that torture happens in war. But we defended the official position of our nation against torture and believed it our duty to use our authority to suppress such barbarous cruelty.

This personal history reflects the values that once prevailed throughout the officer corps of the United States Army. It is from this perspective that I found myself both surprised and horrified that our highest governing bodies had sanctioned torture in the interrogations of prisoners during the war on terror. Just one argument was given in favor of torture: it provides us with useful information. This was, of course, the very justification given by the Communist jailers for the torture of our men in Vietnam. It was, frankly, hard for me to believe that America would employ such savage logic. In brief, these concerns flashed through my mind:

- The use of torture undermines the moral basis for just war. America has traditionally waged war for the sake of a better peace. Yet torture inspires the kind of hatred that I felt as a boy for the North Vietnamese. America has traditionally understood that behind the military conflict is a battle for hearts and minds. But how can we fight terror—which is rooted in hatred—when we are torturing the fathers, sons, and brothers of an already hate-filled enemy? The reality is that how we treat prisoners of war is directly related to the justice of our cause in war. And the justice of our cause in war is always a matter of strategic as well as moral significance.
- The use of torture wrongly assumes that the ends justify the means. But this is contrary to our entire national tradition. Is it no longer true, as my grandfather insisted, that by embracing the evil of our enemies we have already been defeated? Does not the use of torture change us into the image of our enemies? How can we now deny the charge of barbarism when we ruthlessly apply violence to human beings who are

no longer capable of doing us harm? How will we gain the respect of the world community—so important for future peace—if we conduct ourselves like savages?

- The sanction of torture betrays the military's moral obligation to ensure the ethical development of our soldiers. Do senior officers no longer have a moral duty to oversee the character formation of their troops? Do we consider what it must be like for our soldiers to be trained and commanded to perform these heinous acts of torture, as if they were not themselves victims of these savage acts? What horrors will we unleash on our civilian society when military torturers are returned to their families and neighborhoods?

With these concerns, I seek to highlight the moral and ethical issues at stake in the matter of torture. On every level, government-sanctioned torture is a disgrace to the American military tradition and a betrayal of the values cherished by this country for every generation before our own.

All these concerns summarize my abhorrence for torture as a patriotic American soldier (I served for thirteen years before resigning as a major to enter the gospel ministry). But as a Christian, I find that my revulsion against this policy becomes even deeper. From this perspective, I was especially grieved to learn that the Bush administration's sanction of waterboarding was publicly defended by evangelical Christian leaders. To my surprise and indignation, instead of applying the obvious implications of the sixth commandment to this situation, Christian leaders lined up in support of their conservative political partners. Was this blind political loyalty, without a biblical conscience? Or does the evangelical support for torture provide yet more evidence that the biblical worldview has eroded not only in the culture but also in our churches? In the 1950s and '60s, it was the liberal churches—those that denied the Bible—that took the moral high ground in the civil-rights movement, while Bible-believers disgraced their cause by supporting racism. Now, in our time, the evangelical movement is engaging in a similar betrayal of God's Word by endorsing torture while liberal theologians and churches take the high ground in opposition. In this way, we may measure the spiritual catastrophe taking place with respect to the conservative Christian support of waterboarding. How will Bible-believing Christians provide a morally persuasive witness to the dignity of human life when our leaders are racing forward to endorse the torture of divine image-bearers who are providentially placed at our mercy? How will our secular society be drawn to the Bible as the holy Word of God when they see its representatives giving public support to such an obvious moral evil as torture?

In this context, I am grateful for J. Porter Harlow's study *How Should We Treat Detainees?* There are few greater needs today than for Christians to think with biblical clarity on important moral topics. This book looks at the details, practical and historical, of a particular issue: waterboarding. In advance of this fine study, I urge us to start with a clear understanding of God's sixth commandment and its impact on our treatment of fellow human beings. Christians have historically understood that God's command "You shall not murder" carries with it a positive duty to preserve human life and well-being. Clearly, this command does not rule out just war or the bearing of the sword for civil justice (Rom. 13:4), since God himself commands both just combat and capital punishment. But neither of these exceptions to our calling to preserve life is in view when it comes to the torture of prisoners. A prisoner of war is no longer a combatant. He may desire to inflict future harm on our soldiers and nation. But by virtue of his imprisonment, a captive is no longer a threat to do violence. Christians must realize that God's own moral standard requires us to preserve the life and health of human beings under our care. These and other vital issues are given careful treatment in this worthy book. I especially commend Harlow's treatment of the vital issue of man in the image of God. Here is a priority that Christians must recover for its implications to a wide range of ethical topics, not least of which is that of torture.

Christians today live in a culture that is increasingly calloused toward precious human life. Against this "culture of death" we bear a pro-life witness on behalf of the God of love. The harm to this witness is incalculable when the passions of terrorism and war so cloud Christians' judgment that we lose our moral compass. This is precisely what has happened, I believe, in the Christian support of torture. May God bless this volume in its witness to God's moral law, to the dignity of all human life in the image of God, and to the restoration of biblical discernment among God's people for the pressing ethical questions of our times.

Richard D. Phillips
Senior Minister, Second Presbyterian Church
Greenville, South Carolina
July 2016

Preface

In the spring of 2008, I was in my first year of teaching international law as part of the Master of Laws program at the U.S. Army's Judge Advocate General's School in Charlottesville, Virginia. I was developing a one credit elective that would examine war crimes prosecutions since World War II, and I decided to finish the elective by inviting a prosecutor from the military commissions at Naval Base Guantanamo to be a guest speaker. I invited Marine Lieutenant Colonel Stuart Couch because we had met years before during a court-martial when I was a trial attorney at a Marine Corps Base in Eastern North Carolina. I knew Stuart Couch's reputation as a prosecutor's prosecutor, a strong advocate for the Government who I did not believe had ever served as a defense counsel during his long career as a trial attorney. I expected him to come and talk to my students about bringing justice to terrorists.

I was astonished when Couch came and explained his refusal to prosecute Mohamedou Ould Slahi, an accused al-Qaeda operative suspected of assembling the terrorist cell that included one of the September 11th hijackers.[1] In what he has characterized as the toughest decision of his career,[2] Couch had determined that Slahi's confessions had been obtained by the U.S. Government as the result of torture, which made them inadmissible in a court according to international and domestic law.[3]

[1] Jess Bravin, "The Conscience of the Colonel," *Wall Street Journal*, March 31, 2007, http://www.wsj.com/articles/ SB117529704337355155.

[2] Ibid.

[3] Convention against Torture and Other Cruel, Inhuman or Degrading

Ever since the pictures had emerged from Abu Ghraib in 2003, I had heard the news media repeat allegations that the U.S. Government was purposefully torturing and mistreating detainees, but my limited experience with detainees in Iraq and all my training as a Marine Officer had led me to be skeptical of the allegations and to believe that alleged detainee mistreatment was the result of individual misconduct rather than U.S. Government policy. Yet having heard Couch—a self described Republican and evangelical Christian—say that the U.S. Government had obtained evidence using torture, I was forced to reconsider all of my assumptions.

But even more astonishing than his legal objection to prosecuting Slahi was the fact that Couch told my class of military lawyers that he had a moral objection to the torture and cruel treatment of Slahi. I was challenged by his description of torture as a violation of the image of God in man since I—also an evangelical Christian from a confessional, Reformed Church—had not been thoughtful enough to struggle with this issue before.

The year 2008 was also my first year of seminary studies at Reformed Theological Seminary in Washington, D.C. For the next seven years, I considered the issue of detainee treatment from my position as a Christian and as an international and operational law attorney in the Marine Corps. In 1 Corinthians 10:31, Paul writes that Christians should glorify God in whatever activity they are engaged. Therefore, Christians should be able to wage war to the glory of God, which implies that Christians should not employ methods of warfare (e.g., methods of interrogation) that fall short of the glory of God. But I was unsure whether any of the Bush administration's enhanced interrogation techniques fell short of the glory of God. This book has been a labor to explore the limits of righteous warfare and to determine if any of the interrogation methods used by

---

Treatment or Punishment, art. 15, 1465 U.N.T.S. 85, at 116, Article 15; U.S. Const. amend. V.

the United States during the years 2002–6 crossed the line and fell short of the glory of God.

This book is not about whether the U.S. tortured detainees. Torture is a legal term not a Scriptural term. This book is about whether waterboarding and other methods that the U.S. used to interrogate detainees violated biblical requirements and the just war tradition's standards that reflect those biblical requirements.

J. Porter Harlow
Fairfax, Virginia
July 2016

Acknowledgements

I would like to express the greatest respect and appreciation for Dr. Howard Griffith, who was not only a source of great encouragement and wise counsel in his role as my faculty advisor for this work, but he has also been a father in the faith as he has led me into a deeper appreciation for my union with Jesus Christ in his death and resurrection. Dr. Griffith's discussions of John Murray's *Redemption Accomplished and Applied* and Romans chapter 6 have changed my life forever.

I would also like to express my appreciation and respect to the entire faculty and staff of Reformed Theological Seminary, Washington, D.C., for their teaching and encouragement, especially Dr. Chad Van Dixhoorn, Dr. Scott Redd, Geoff Sackett, Dr. Peter Lee, and Jennifer McGahey, who were all very generous with their time as well as their advice on this project.

I would like to acknowledge the great debt that I owe to the work of Paul Ramsey and James Turner Johnson. While there are many books and scholarly articles on *jus ad bellum*, the branch of the just war tradition concerned with starting wars justly, I have found few theologians and philosophers who have dealt with the methods of warfare that are the subject of the *jus in bello* branch and the concern of military service members whose profession is to employ those methods. Dr. Johnson had never met me when he received an e-mail from me, so he was very kind to answer me and then correspond with me, answering my questions about the implications of his writings with regard to interrogations. I hope that this work would be found to be walking in their footsteps.

I also owe a great debt to J. Daryl Charles, who also had never met me before I e-mailed him, but who took hours out of his teaching and speaking schedules to correspond with me in many e-mails and to talk with me on several long phone calls.

I would like to thank the seminary libraries in the Washington Theological Consortium, especially the librarians at Virginia Theological Seminary's Bishop Payne Library in Alexandria, Virginia. I wrote most of this book in the VTS library, and I pulled most of the books in the bibliography from its shelves. It is one of my favorite places in this world to write. I would also like to thank Mr. Michael Farrell, the Library Director at Reformed Theological Seminary, Orlando, for his assistance in obtaining several hard to find articles.

I would like to express my appreciation for my pastor and our church's local theologian, Charlie Baile, for his friendship and his comments on this project. He has taught me how to love the church through his advice and his example.

I would also like to thank John J. Hughes and Amanda Martin at P&R Publishing for their kindness and indispensable assistance in publishing this project.

Finally, I would like to thank my wife, Cathy, and our three wonderful children, Andrew, Grace and Calvin, for their love, encouragement and patience over the last several years while I have been working on this. The Lord has blessed me greatly through each one of you individually and as a family. I am enjoying our sojourn through this world together.

Introduction

Prior to 2002, U.S. practice was that all persons captured on the battlefield received at least the baseline protections in Common Article 3 of the Geneva Conventions of 1949.[1] That practice changed in 2002 when President Bush decided that Taliban and al-Qaeda detainees would not receive any protections from the Geneva Conventions.[2] President Bush's decision effectively put these detainees into a legal vacuum while they were at their most vulnerable point—bound in the hands of their enemies whose nation had recently suffered a terrible act of terror.

Once the limits of the law of war were removed, the Department of Defense[3] and the Central Intelligence Agency[4] approved the use of

[1] Hamdan v. Rumsfeld, 548 U.S. 557 (2006).

[2] George W. Bush, Memo, "Humane Treatment of Taliban and al Qaeda Detainees" (Feb. 7, 2002), http://nsarchive.gwu.edu/NSAEBB/NSAEBB127/02.02.07.pdf.

[3] Donald Rumsfeld, "Counter Resistance Techniques" (Dec. 2, 2002), http://nsarchive.gwu.edu/torturingdemocracy /documents/20021127-1.pdf ; James T. Hill, "Counter-Resistance Techniques" (Oct. 25, 2002), http://nsarchive. gwu.edu /torturingdemocracy/documents/20021025.pdf; Major General Michael Dunlavey, "Counter-Resistance Strategies" (Oct. 11, 2002), http://nsarchive.gwu.edu/torturingdemocracy/documents/20021011.pdf; Jay S. Bybee, Memo, "Interrogation of al Qaeda Operative" (Aug 1, 2002): 3–4, http://nsarchive.gwu.edu/torturingdemocracy/ documents/20020122.pdf.

[4] Steven G. Bradbury, Memo "Application of United States Obligations Under Article 16 of the Convention Against Torture to Certain Techniques that May Be Used in the Interrogation of High Value al Qaeda Detainees" (May 30, 2005): 7, http://nsarchive.gwu.edu/torture_archive/docs/Bradbury%20memo.pdf.

new enhanced interrogation techniques. Those techniques were above and beyond those that had been previously available to interrogators in the Army Interrogation Manual.[5] Those enhanced interrogation techniques remained available to the Department of Defense until 2006 when the U.S. Congress passed the McCain Amendment into law, prohibiting the military from using any interrogation techniques not available in the U.S. Army Manual. And they remained available to the CIA until President Obama signed an executive order that provided the same limits as those on the military.[6]

The public record shows that Christians serving in the military from 2002–6 were concerned about the morality of the interrogation techniques that were being used against detainees. One found an answer in the Psalms and the just war tradition.[7] Another sought counsel from his brother-in-law, an evangelical theologian, and ultimately came under conviction through the words of his priest spoken during the liturgy at the Falls Church[8] on a Sunday morning when he was struggling with the issue.[9]

[5] Department of the Army, "Field Manual 34–52 Intelligence Interrogation" (Sept 1992) https://www.loc.gov/rr/frd/Military_Law/pdf/intel_interrrogation_sept-1992.pdf. This Field Manual on interrogations was later superseded, in 2006, by Department of the Army, "Field Manual 2-22.3 Human Intelligence Collector Operations" (Sept 2006) http://armypubs.army.mil/doctrine/DR_pubs/dr_a/pdf/fm2_22x3.pdf.

[6] Exec. Order No. 13491, 3 C.F.R. 199 (2009).

[7] Redacted Name, e-mail from an Army Officer in the Fourth Infantry Division (Aug. 14, 2003), https://www.aclu.org/files/projects/foiasearch/pdf/DOD002818.pdf.

[8] The Falls Church was an Episcopal Church outside Washington, D.C., where some evangelical Christians who worked in President Bush's administration worshipped. The church has since become part of the Anglican Church in North America (ACNA).

[9] Lindsey Wagner, "Former Guantanamo Bay Prosecutor Shares Story," *University of Virginia School of Law* (Feb. 19, 2009) http://www.law.virginia.edu/html/news/2009_spr/colonel.htm.

The essential issues for many Christians were: When the law is removed as a limit on the state's authority over a prisoner, what will fill the vacuum? To what authority can national security leaders, soldiers, and interrogators turn when they have doubts about the morality of interrogation techniques that they are involved in or observe? What does Scripture or the historic just war tradition say, if anything, about the treatment of wartime detainees?

This book will argue that waterboarding and other enhanced interrogation techniques approved by the U.S. Government during the years 2002–6 were contrary to the teachings of the just war tradition and the Scriptures it reflects. This book will try to demonstrate that the love of neighbor taught by Jesus Christ[10] provides the "twin-born"[11] justification for and limitation upon warfare. It justifies engaging in righteous warfare to protect our neighbors while also providing the limitation on righteous warfare that protects noncombatants such as prisoners and the civilian population from harm. This book will also argue that Christians should have recognized that the law's limits on the treatment of detainees should not have been removed based upon the dishonorableness of the enemy's conduct prior to his capture. The limits should have been maintained based upon the potential for evil in the heart of the captor who is a fallen person prone to sin.

Chapter 1 will provide a factual background by documenting the U.S. Government's approval and use of enhanced interrogation techniques. That chapter will group them according to the following effects: (1) pain and physical abuse, (2) sexual exploitation, (3) religious exploitation, (4) assaults on reason using extreme sensory deprivation, sleep deprivation, and isolation, and (5) the denial of human dignity through the treatment of detainees like animals.

[10] Luke 10:25–37.

[11] Paul Ramsey, *The Just War: Force and Political Responsibility* (Lanham, MD: Rowman & Littlefield Publishers, Inc., 2002), 144.

Chapter 2 will provide a brief background on the just war tradition and how it came to be reasserted during the twentieth century as a backlash against the philosophy of realism and the atrocities perpetrated against noncombatants during World Wars I and II, the threat of nuclear annihilation during the Cold War, and as a justification and limitation during the war of counterinsurgency in Vietnam. Most importantly, chapter 2 will establish the two *jus in bello* principles of (1) discrimination and (2) proportionality that this book will apply to the use of enhanced interrogation techniques as a method of warfare.

Chapter 3 will argue that discrimination is the deontological principle that requires the state to distinguish between combatants and noncombatants. Discrimination provides the twin-born justification and limitation on methods of warfare: permitting attacks on combatants while requiring that prisoners be treated as noncombatants who are to be respected and protected while in detention. The state should discriminate in this way because Jesus discriminates in this way. Jesus is both the Warrior King in command of heaven's armies[12] as well as the merciful Savior calling upon all people to love their neighbor,[13] love their enemy,[14] protect the powerless in their society,[15] and show mercy to prisoners.[16]

Chapter 4 will argue that proportionality is the principle that considers whether the method of warfare is proportional to the end that is being sought. When applied to the U.S. Government's interrogation techniques discussed in chapter 1, Christians should find that those techniques are never proportional to any end sought because they assault the *Imago Dei* in the detainee as well as the Image of Christ in the Christian who approves the technique or uses the technique.

[12] Rev. 19:11–16.

[13] Luke 10:25–37.

[14] Matt. 5:43–45.

[15] Ex. 22:21–23.

[16] Matt. 25:31–46 as a specific issue representing a generalized good to be done for all persons. Gal. 6:10.

Chapter 5 will review the dirty hands scenarios in which a ticking time bomb is hidden in a city, threatening many lives, and a leader must choose whether or not to torture the prisoner who knows the bomb's location. The chapter will argue that ticking time bomb scenarios are intellectual frauds[17] that present unrealistically certain facts with artificially limited options that fail to account for the intervention of a sovereign God or His blessing upon other righteous efforts to stop the bomb. The chapter will critique the argument of some Christians who believe that leaders must sometimes take immoral actions and dirty their hands with sin in order to protect national security. Chapter 5 will argue that Christians should not accept dirty hands or theological positions that accept dirty hands.

Chapter 6 will review the clean hands scenario of two evangelical theologians who believe that Scripture warrants the state's use of pain for interrogational purposes. Chapter 6 will argue that their position fails to make a persuasive case for expanding the authority of the state's sword in Romans 13:3–4 beyond the express purpose of being an instrument for punishment.

Finally, this book will conclude that Christians should adopt a biblical worldview on this critical topic. Christians should not be shaped by the utilitarian, realist, or political patterns of this world. They should be shaped by the transforming and renewing of their minds that comes from wrestling with God's word to discern the character of God and what He finds good and acceptable and perfect.[18] Christians should also recognize that removing the law of war's protections in Common Article 3 was not wise because of the usefulness of laws in restraining evil and revealing what is pleasing to God so that Christians may serve him with righteousness.

This book will demonstrate that the public record is unfortunately replete with evangelical Christians defending the use of scrip-

[17] David Luban, "Liberalism, Torture, and the Ticking Time Bomb," *Virginia Law Review* 94 (2005): 1425.

[18] Rom. 12:2.

turally objectionable interrogation techniques. They did so using utilitarian modes of reasoning, Christian versions of Realism, and Scripture. The author hopes to provide a faithful response that will cause Christians to wrestle with Scripture and come to their own faithful conclusions before the techniques are used again. Otherwise, Christian national security officials and military service members in the future will encounter this issue again, wonder how they should treat the enemy, and look to how Christians answered these questions in the past. This book is offered to honor their service to our Lord and the rulers to whom He has given the sword.[19] It is my prayer that He will bless them with wisdom as they wield it on His behalf.

[19] Rom. 13:4.

1

How Did the U.S. Treat Detainees?

We tortured [Mohammed al-] Qahtani...His treatment met the legal definition of torture.[1]

During the beginning of the wars in Afghanistan and Iraq, Americans heard conflicting news reports about the treatment of detainees captured on those battlefields. In 2004, Christians saw the pictures from Abu Ghraib, but in 2005 they heard President Bush, the president who identified himself as an evangelical Christian, say, "We do not torture."[2] Then in 2008, John Kiriakou told the media that he had participated in the waterboarding of detainee Abu Zubayda as the CIA Chief of Counterterrorist Operations in Pakistan, and that he had come to regard waterboarding as torture since then.[3] Many Christians struggled to make sense of the insensible.

[1] This quotation is from Susan Crawford, who was appointed during President Bush's administration as the Convening Authority for the Military Commissions. Bob Woodward, "Detainee Tortured, Says U.S. Official" *Washington Post*, Jan. 14, 2009, http://www. washingtonpost.com/wp-dyn/content/article/2009/01/13/AR20090113 03372.html.

[2] Deb Riechmann, "Bush Declares: 'We Do Not Torture'" *Washington Post*, November 7, 2005 http://www.washingtonpost.com/wp-dyn/content/article/2005/11/07/AR2005110700521_pf.html.

[3] Joby Warrick and Dan Eggen, "Waterboarding Recounted," *Washington Post*, December 11, 2007, http://www. washingtonpost.com/wp-dyn/content/article/2007/12/10/AR2007121002091.html.

Christians had two recurring questions: how were detainees being treated and—not whether that treatment was necessarily torture—but was the treatment biblically objectionable? Many evangelical Christians try to live their lives with a biblical worldview, believing that they should apply biblical wisdom to everything in life.[4] For those involved in national security or military service, that means bringing a biblical worldview to their jobs.

One such person was Marine Lieutenant Colonel Stuart Couch. Couch characterized himself as an evangelical Christian[5] and a Republican[6] from North Carolina. He had been a Marine KC-130 pilot prior to going to law school and becoming a prosecutor in the Marine Corps. After 9/11, Couch found out that one of his former squadron mates, Michael 'Rocks' Horrocks, had been one of the pilots of Airline flight 175 that hit the South Tower of the World Trade Center.[7] Couch jumped at the opportunity when he was asked whether he wanted to be one of the prosecutors at the military commissions. There he was put in charge of prosecuting the detainees held at Guantanamo Bay, Cuba, who were suspected of planning the September 11th attacks such as Mohamedou Ould Slahi and Mohammed al-Qahtani.[8] Couch kept a picture of Rocks' widow and children on his desk to remind him of the importance of his task.

Couch had his first doubts about the morality of the U.S. treatment of detainees during his first visit to the Guantanamo Bay prison.

[4] First Corinthians 10:31 provides the exhortation for Christians to do all things and think all things to the glory of God. From this verse and others, the Westminster Divines drafted the first answer in the Westminster Shorter Catechism: The chief end of man is to glorify God and enjoy him forever.

[5] Stuart Couch, Interview, *Torturing Democracy*, National Security Archive (October 9, 2007), http://nsarchive.gwu.edu/torturingdemocracy/interviews/stuart_couch.html.

[6] Jess Bravin, *Terror Courts* (New Haven, CT: Yale University Press, 2013), 382.

[7] Ibid., 7.

[8] Couch, Interview, http://nsarchive.gwu.edu/torturingdemocracy/interviews/stuart_couch.html.

While entering a room from which he was going to watch a detainee interrogation, he heard loud heavy metal music blaring from another room nearby.[9] When Couch went down the hall to tell the personnel to turn the music down, he saw a detainee shackled in a stress position with his feet and hands shackled together on the floor.[10] He also saw that the room was pitch black except for a strobe light that was flashing.[11] Couch perceived that the detainee was praying and that his lips were moving. Immediately, two civilians stepped into the doorway to block Couch from coming in. Couch was shocked because the strobe light, the heavy metal music[12] and the stress position reminded him of his experience as a pilot when he was sent to SERE training, which was to prepare U.S. pilots to resist interrogation techniques that had been employed against American Prisoners of War (POWs) by their captors during the Korean and Vietnam Wars. Couch has said, "I started having some serious misgivings about what was going on."[13]

Couch's misgivings were confirmed as he prepared to prosecute the case of Mohamedou Ould Slahi. Slahi was suspected of being a key orchestrator of the al-Qaeda cell in Europe that supplied the hijackers for the attacks on 9/11.[14] In reviewing the evidence against Slahi, Couch wondered why Slahi had refused to cooperate with interrogators for an extensive period of time, then without explanation started providing pages and pages of written confessions and information about al-Qaeda. Knowing that a Prosecutor has a legal and ethical duty to provide a defense counsel with evidence associated with any interrogation, Couch researched the treatment of Slahi by

[9] Couch heard a song titled "Let the Bodies Hit the Floor" by the band Drowning Pool. Bravin, *Terror Courts*, 84.

[10] Ibid.

[11] Ibid.

[12] Couch, Interview, http://nsarchive.gwu.edu/torturingdemocracy/interviews/stuart_couch.html.

[13] Ibid.

[14] Ibid.

interrogators. Couch discovered many things which are now part of the public record.

The U.S. Senate Armed Services Committee (SASC) examined the treatment of Slahi and found that a Defense Intelligence Agency (DIA) interrogation plan for Slahi, which was approved by Secretary of Defense Rumsfeld, described breaking down Slahi's ego using the following methods:

- Ridiculing him,
- Making him wear a mask,
- Making him wear signs that said in Arabic "liar," "coward," and "dog,"
- Treating him like a dog by putting a collar on him, making him bark, and making him perform tricks,
- Treating him as a woman by forcing him to wear a burqa, and
- Strip searching him, not for security reasons, but to assault his modesty.[15]

The SASC also determined that the DIA plan described exploiting Slahi's religious convictions using the following methods:

- Denying his opportunity to pray,
- Having a female interrogator engage in close physical contact, and
- Playing music to stress Slahi because he believed music is forbidden by Islam.[16]

The DIA plan also described the intent to reduce all outside stimuli in order to isolate and disorient Slahi by shackling Slahi to the floor in a

[15] Senate Committee on Armed Services, "Inquiry into the Treatment of Detainees in U.S. Custody," 136, Nov 20, 2008, http://www.armed-services.senate.gov/imo/media/doc/Detainee-Report-Final_April-22-2009.pdf.

[16] Ibid.

completely white interrogation room with sealed doors to block outside light, the use of strobe lights, and the continuous playing of heavy metal rock music such as the band Drowning Pool's song, "Let the Bodies Hit the Floor."[17]

In one incident during his interrogation, a masked interrogator told Slahi that the interrogator had a dream where he saw four detainees that were chained together at the feet. They dug a hole that was six feet long, six feet deep, and four feet wide. Then he observed the detainees throw a plain, unpainted, pine casket with the number 760, which was Slahi's internment serial number, on the ground.[18] The interrogator told Slahi that "beatings and physical pain are not the worst thing in the world. After all, after being beaten for a while, humans tend to disconnect the mind from the body and make it through. However, there are worse things than physical pain."[19] The interrogator told Slahi that he would "very soon disappear down a very dark hole. His very existence will become erased . . . no one will know what happened to him and, eventually, no one will care."[20] In another incident, an interrogator showed Slahi a false letter stating that, because of Slahi's failure to cooperate, his mother had been detained[21] and was being brought to Guantanamo where the authorities feared for her safety around so many male detainees.[22] Couch understood that to be a threat to have Slahi's mother raped.[23]

The cumulative effect of Slahi's treatment drove him mad. The Schmidt-Furlow Report found where an interrogator wrote to an Army psychologist that "Slahi told me he is 'hearing voices' now...He

[17] Ibid; Bravin, *Terror Courts*, 84.

[18] Bravin, *Terror Courts*, 106.

[19] Lieutenant General Randall Schmidt and Brigadier General John Furlow, "Investigation into FBI Allegations of Detainee Abuse at Guantanamo Bay, Cuba Detention Facility," 25, June 9, 2005, http://nsarchive.gwu.edu/torturingdemocracy/documents/20050400.pdf.

[20] Ibid.

[21] Ibid.

[22] Bravin, *Terror Courts*, 106–7.

[23] Ibid., 142.

is worried as he knows this is not normal....By the way...is this something that happens to people who have little external stimulus such as daylight, human interaction etc???? Seems creepy."[24] The Army psychologist responded that sensory deprivation can cause hallucinations because "[i]n the dark you create things out of what little you have."[25]

The Objections of an Evangelical Christian Prosecutor

Marine Lieutenant Colonel Couch, Slahi's prosecutor, determined that he had two objections to the treatment of Slahi that would cause him to refuse to participate in the prosecution of the case. First, as a lawyer, Couch had a legal objection to the treatment of Slahi since the treatment violated the Convention Against Torture and other Cruel, Inhuman, or Degrading Treatment[26] as well as a U.S. criminal statute known as the War Crimes Act.[27]

Second, Couch determined that the treatment was morally objectionable.[28] Couch had previously discussed his spiritual misgivings with his brother-in-law, Bill Wilder, an evangelical theologian at the Center for Christian Study in Charlottesville, Virginia. Then one Sunday, while participating in the liturgy for a baptism at the Falls Church in Northern Virginia, Couch was initially distracted from the worship service by his thoughts on the Slahi case.[29] While mechani-

[24] Senate Committee on Armed Services, "Inquiry into the Treatment of Detainees in U.S. Custody," 140–41.

[25] Ibid., 141.

[26] The U.S. Senate ratified the Convention against torture and other cruel, inhuman or degrading treatment or punishment (CAT), and the CAT entered into force in the U.S. on November 20, 1994. In prohibiting the use of torture, cruel, inhuman and degrading treatment, Article 2 expressly prohibits exceptions during wartime. Article 15 would exclude the statements Slahi made from being used against him in court.

[27] War Crimes Act of 1996, 18 U.S.C. § 2441 (1996).

[28] Bravin, *Terror Courts*, 153.

[29] Ibid., 148.

cally participating in the liturgy, the words caught his attention. The priest asked the congregation, "Will you seek and serve Christ in all persons, loving your neighbor as yourself?" "I will with God's help," the congregation responded. Couch realized that "all persons" included Mohamedou Ould Slahi.[30]

Next, the priest asked the congregation, "Will you strive for justice and peace among all people, and respect the dignity of every human being?" Couch already believed that all human beings are created in the image of God and that they were due a certain amount of respect whether or not they acknowledged being made in the image of their creator.[31] Couch already believed that Christians honored God by observing certain boundaries in the treatment of persons even if they had acted contrary to the image of God in them.[32] But participating in worship on this particular Sunday, Couch was particularly moved when he responded, "I will with God's help." Couch later described the priest's words as "a thunderclap to the side of the face."[33] He said, "I felt at that moment that I was shaken to my innermost being, that this was a bigger issue and I had to do something."[34] Two days later, Couch told the Chief Prosecutor at the military commissions, retired Army Colonel Bob Swann, that he had legal and moral objections to further participation in the prosecution of Slahi.[35]

[30] Ibid., 149.

[31] Ibid., 146.

[32] Couch, "Interview," Oct. 9, 2007, http://nsarchive.gwu.edu/torturingdemocracy/interviews/stuart_couch.html.

[33] Ibid.

[34] Ibid. Lindsey Wagner, "Former Guantanamo Bay Prosecutor Shares Story,"

[34] Lindsey Wagner, "Former Guantanamo Bay Prosecutor Shares Story," *University of Virginia School of Law* (Feb. 19, 2009), http://www.law.virginia.edu/html/news/2009_spr/colonel.htm.

[35] Bravin, *Terror Courts*, 151.

The Fateful Decision That No Law Applied

On February 7, 2002, President Bush made the fateful decision that no law—international or domestic—set a standard of protection for the al-Qaeda and Taliban detainees.[36] The memo has been called the "original sin" that opened the gate to the enhanced interrogation techniques used by the Department of Defense (DoD) and the Central Intelligence Agency (CIA)[37] as well as the many subsequent, unapproved acts of detainee abuse that were done under the belief that no law applied.

That decision was a significant break from traditional U.S. doctrine. Prior to 2002, the U.S. policy had been that Common Article 3 of the Geneva Conventions of 1949 was a bottom floor of protection for all persons captured by their enemies on the battlefield regardless of whether that person was a lawful combatant (e.g., a member of a state's armed force) or unprivileged belligerent (e.g., a non-state fighter).[38] That was the belief of Secretary of State Colin Powell, former Chairman of the Joint Chiefs of Staff,[39] the teaching of the U.S. Army's Judge Advocate General's Legal Center and School,[40] and the legal rulings from the International Court of Justice[41] and the

[36] George W. Bush, "Humane Treatment of Taliban and al Qaeda Detainees," Feb. 7, 2002, http://nsarchive.gwu.edu/NSAEBB/NSAEBB127/02.02.07.pdf.

[37] Mark Danner, "Abu Ghraib: The Hidden Story," *New York Review of Books*, Oct. 7, 2004, http://www.nybooks. com/articles/2004/10/07/abu-ghraib-the-hidden-story/.

[38] Hamdan v. Rumsfeld, 548 U.S. 557, 631 (2006); Colin Powell, "Draft Memorandum for the President on the Applicability of the Geneva Conventions to the Conflict in Afghanistan" (Jan. 26, 2002), http://nsarchive.gwu.edu/torturingdemocracy/documents/20020126.pdf.

[39] Powell, "Draft Memorandum for the President."

[40] Hamdan v. Rumsfeld, 548 U.S. 557, 631n63 (2006) (quoting the U.S. Army Judge Advocate General's Legal Center and School, Law of War Handbook (2004), page 144, for the principle that Common Article 3 "serves as a 'minimum yardstick of protection' in all conflicts").

[41] Nicaragua v. United States, 1986 International Court of Justice 14, 218,

International Criminal Tribunal for the Former Yugoslavia.[42] President Bush appeared to acknowledge the break with the past when he called for "new thinking in the law of war."[43]

While the world has focused on the issue of torture, Common Article 3 prohibits much more than that. Common Article 3 prohibits "violence against the person . . . cruel treatment and torture" as well as "outrages upon personal dignity, particularly humiliating and degrading treatment."[44] Common Article 3 is a separate "mini-convention"[45] that provides a bottom floor of protection, but it does not provide the much greater protections that a prisoner of war would get from the Third Geneva Convention or that a civilian internee would get from the Fourth Geneva Convention.

So from President Bush's decision in 2002 until the U.S. Supreme Court caused him to reverse that position 2006,[46] the U.S. legal position on the applicability of Common Article 3 protections took a detour into lawlessness. In removing the protections of Common Article 3, the President removed the law designed to protect detainees in the hands of their enemies. In its place, the 2002 memo made a bare statement of policy that detainees should be treated humanely unless inconsistent with military necessity.

> As a matter of policy, the United States Armed Forces shall continue to treat detainees humanely and, to the extent ap-

---

25 I.L.M. 1023.

[42] Prosecutor v. Tadic, Case No. IT-94-1, Decision on the Defence Motion for Interlocutory Appeal on Jurisdiction, 102 (International Criminal Tribunal for the former Yugoslavia Appellate Chamber, Oct. 2, 199).

[43] Bush, "Humane Treatment of Taliban and al Qaeda Detainees."

[44] Common Article 3 of the Geneva Conventions of 1949.

[45] William H. Boothby, *The Law of Targeting* (Oxford, Oxford University Press: 2012), 430.

[46] President Bush's decision was effectively reversed by the U.S. Supreme Court's 2006 decision in Hamdan v. Rumsfeld, 548 U.S. 557, 631 (2006).

> propriate and consistent with military necessity, in a manner consistent with the principles of Geneva.[47]

Essentially, the President placed the detainees in a legal vacuum where their only protection was a policy that the President or presumably a subordinate could waive if he determined that military necessity trumped humane treatment.

Removing the legal applicability opened the door to the administration's enhanced interrogation techniques that were used by DoD and the CIA. On December 2, 2002, Secretary of Defense Donald Rumsfeld approved the immediate use or availability of the following counter-resistance techniques to be used for the interrogation of detainees at Guantanamo Bay:

- Waterboarding "to induce the misperception of suffocation."
- Use of scenarios "designed to convince the detainee that death or severely painful consequences are imminent for him and/or his family."
- Exposure to cold and water.
- Physical assaults and batteries such as grabbing, poking, and pushing.
- Stress positions.
- Isolation for up to 30 days with extensions available upon approval of the Commanding General.
- Deprivation of light and auditory stimuli.
- Twenty-hour interrogations.
- Removal of religious and comfort items.
- Removal of clothing.
- Forced grooming (shaving of religious beards).
- The use of phobias to scare the detainees (e.g., fear of dogs).[48]

[47] Bush, "Humane Treatment of Taliban and al Qaeda Detainees."

[48] Donald Rumsfeld, "Counter Resistance Techniques" (Dec. 2, 2002), http://nsarchive.gwu.edu/torturingdemocracy /documents/20021127-1.pdf;

The approval of this list, arguably intended by Rumsfeld to be treatment less than torture, opened another gate to arguably unintended consequences when interrogators combined the techniques and used them over an extended period of time, such as they did to Mohammed al-Qahtani, which resulted in treatment that the Bush administration appointee in charge of the military commissions at Guantanamo Bay had to admit was "torture."[49]

U.S. Government intelligence officials suspected that al-Qahtani would have been the 20th hijacker on 9/11 but for a suspicious customs agent who denied him entry into the U.S.[50] The interrogation of al-Qahtani included 160 consecutive days of isolation during which he was interrogated 18 hours a day for 48 of 54 days, exposed to cold for prolonged periods of time, forced to stand naked in front of a female interrogator, threatened with a dog named Zeus, forced to wear a woman's bra on his head, forced to wear thong underwear on his head, tied to a leash and forced to perform dog tricks, and forced to endure insults against his mother and sister, including the insult that they were "whores."[51] As a result of the sleep deprivation and the extreme temperatures, al-Qahtani was hospitalized twice with life-threatening bradycardia, a condition where his heart rate dropped as low as 35 beats per minute.[52] As for his mental state, he was observed crouching in the corner of his cell, hearing voices and talking to non-existent people.[53] The convening authority for the military commissions, who had served in the President Reagan and first President Bush's administrations, had to stop al-Qahtani's commissions case

---

James T. Hill, "Counter-Resistance Techniques" (Oct. 25, 2002), http://nsarchive. gwu.edu/torturingdemocracy/documents/20021025.pdf; Major General Michael Dunlavey, "Counter-Resistance Strategies" (Oct. 11, 2002), http://nsarchive.gwu.edu/torturingdemocracy/documents/20021011.pdf.

[49] Woodward, "Detainee Tortured, Says U.S. Official."

[50] Ibid.

[51] Ibid.

[52] Ibid.

[53] Ibid.

from going to trial because, "His treatment met the legal definition of torture."[54]

Summary of U.S. Treatment

This book groups detainee interrogation techniques into the following categories: (1) the use of pain and physical abuse, (2) sexual exploitation, (3) religious exploitation, (4) assaults on reason through the use of sleep deprivation, sensory deprivation and isolation, and (5) the denial of human dignity by treating the detainee as an animal.

Pain and Physical Abuse

Pain can be considered in two categories: (1) the officially authorized use of pain and (2) the unapproved yet apparently systematic use of pain and physical abuse as an interrogation technique. Evidence of official physical abuse can be found not only in Secretary Rumsfeld's memo but in the memo from Steven Bradbury, the Principal Deputy Assistant Attorney General in the Department of Justice's Office of Legal Counsel, which documents the ten interrogation techniques that the Central Intelligence Agency considered using against Abu Zubaydah.[55]

Those ten techniques were: (l) attention grasp, (2) walling, (3) facial hold, (4) facial slap (insult slap), (5) cramped confinement, (6) wall standing, (7) stress positions, (8) sleep deprivation, (9) insects placed in a confinement box, and (10) the waterboard.[56] Another

[54] Ibid.

[55] Steven G. Bradbury, "Application of United States Obligations Under Article 16 of the Convention Against Torture to Certain Techniques that May Be Used in the Interrogation of High Value al Qaeda Detainees" (May 30, 2005),
http://nsarchive.gwu.edu/torture_archive/docs/Bradbury%20memo.pdf.

[56] Jay S. Bybee, "Interrogation of al Qaeda Operative," 3–4; Steven G. Bradbury, Memo "Application of United States Obligations Under Article 16 of the Convention Against Torture to Certain Techniques that May Be Used in the Interrogation of High Value al Qaeda Detainees" (May 30, 2005): 7,

memo, by Bush lawyer Jay Bybee, described waterboarding as "the most intense"[57] and the "most traumatic of the enhanced interrogation techniques."[58]

> In this procedure, the individual is bound securely to an inclined bench, which is approximately four feet by seven feet. The individual's feet are generally elevated. A cloth is placed over the forehead and eyes. Water is then [poured on] the cloth in a controlled manner. As this is done, the cloth is lowered until it covers both the nose and mouth. Once the cloth is saturated and completely covers the mouth and nose, air flow is slightly restricted for 20 to 40 seconds due to the presence of the cloth. This causes an increase in carbon dioxide level in the individual's blood. This increase in the carbon dioxide level stimulates increased effort to breathe. This effort plus the cloth produces the perception of suffocation and incipient panic," i.e., the perception of drowning. The individual does not breathe any water into his lungs. During those 20 to 40 seconds, water is continuously [poured] from a height of twelve to twenty-four inches. After this period, the cloth is lifted, and the individual is allowed to breathe unimpeded for three or four full breaths. You have orally informed us that this procedure triggers an automatic physiological sensation of drowning that the individual cannot control even though he may be aware that he is in fact not drowning.[59]

The memo provided the opinion that waterboarding "constitutes a threat of imminent death" because it "creates in the subject the uncontrollable physiological sensation that the subject is drowning."[60]

---

http://nsarchive.gwu.edu/torture_archive/ docs/Bradbury%20memo.pdf.

[57] Ibid., 5.

[58] Ibid., 15.

[59] Ibid., 3–4.

[60] Steven G. Bradbury, Memo "Application of United States Obligations

As the CIA used waterboarding, it induced convulsions and vomiting,[61] and had the effect of leaving Abu Zubayda "completely unresponsive, with bubbles rising from his open, full mouth."[62] Abu Zubayda was reportedly waterboarded 83 times, Khalid Sheikh Mohammed 183 times[63] and Abd al-Rahim al-Nashiri 2 times.[64]

Other examples of the use of pain and physical abuse are widespread. Two detainees were beaten so badly during their detention at Bagram, Afghanistan, that they died from their injuries.[65] LtCol Couch collected reports of detainees in Afghanistan during 2002 being slapped and shoved,[66] a detainee screaming while suspended by his arms as his feet dangled off the ground and soldiers beat him,[67] a detainee whose hands were handcuffed above his head while his face was sprayed with water or pepper,[68] detainees being thrown against walls, and a detainee having an interrogator's finger pressed so deeply under his jawbone that it made him gag.[69] A Department of Defense's Criminal Investigative Task Force (CITF) investigator explained to LtCol Couch that "the intel guys" considered body cavity searches,

---

Under Article 16 of the Convention Against Torture to Certain Techniques that May Be Used in the Interrogation of High Value al Qaeda Detainees," 4.

[61] Senate Select Committee on Intelligence, S. Rep. No. 113-288 at xii (2014), http://www.intelligence.senate.gov/sites/default/files/documents/CRPT-113srpt288.pdf.

[62] Ibid.

[63] Scott Shane, "Waterboarding used 266 times on 2 Suspects" *New York Times*, April 19, 2009, http://www. nytimes.com/2009/04/20/world/20detain.html?_r=0.

[64] Steven G. Bradbury, Memo, "Application of United States Obligations Under Article 16 of the Convention Against Torture to Certain Techniques that May Be Used in the Interrogation of High Value al Qaeda Detainees," 8.

[65] Bravin, *Terror Courts*, 156.

[66] Ibid., 266.

[67] Ibid., 268.

[68] Ibid.

[69] Ibid.

enemas, and rectal penetration a "mechanism to exert control" over detainees about to be interrogated.[70]

Sexual Exploitation

The public record is replete with examples of official and unofficial uses of sexual exploitation as an interrogation technique. Regarding the official uses, the Rumsfeld memo permitted the use of nakedness as a technique and the CIA memo specifically discussed the purposeful use of female interrogators with naked detainees. Furthermore, the military investigation conducted by Lieutenant General Randall Schmidt and Brigadier John General Furlow found an instance where "a female interrogator approached a detainee from behind, rubbed against his back, ran her fingers through his hair, leaned over the detainee touching him on his knee and shoulder and whispered in his ear that his situation was futile.[71] The investigation determined that the technique was an approved technique.[72]

The public record is also replete with reports of the unofficial uses of sexual exploitation as an interrogation technique. The Schmidt-Furlow report found an instance of a female interrogator secretly applying red ink to her hand and then touching a detainee with that hand while telling the detainee that she was menstruating.[73] The detainee responded by throwing himself on the floor and banging his head against it.[74] Ahmed al-Darbi told CITF investigators that he recalled an interrogation in which he was hooded while a female interrogator rubbed his thighs and said she was going to kiss him while a male interrogator on his other side said to Darbi, "I'm going to fuck you."[75] The male interrogator pushed Darbi down on his

[70] Ibid., 156.

[71] Schmidt and Furlow, "Investigation into FBI Allegations of Detainee Abuse at Guantanamo Bay, Cuba Detention Facility."

[72] Ibid.

[73] Ibid.

[74] Ibid.

[75] Bravin, *Terror Courts*, 268.

knees and stood behind Darbi, pretending to anally sodomize him while Darbi moaned.[76] On other occasions, one male interrogator exposed his buttocks, another exposed his penis, and a third showed al-Darbi a condom and said that the interrogator was going to use it while anally sodomizing Darbi.[77]

Religious Exploitation

The overlap between sexual exploitation and religious exploitation is extensive because of the general belief among interrogators that having female interrogators touch a detainee would cause a devout Muslim to feel unclean and unable to pray and thus believe he was cut-off from assistance from his god.[78] In that respect, the threats of sodomy would have a similar effect. A detainee provided to Major General Antonio Taguba's investigation a report that interrogators told him to curse Islam and to thank Jesus that he was alive while they struck the detainee's broken leg.[79] The detainee complied.[80] Al-Qahtani's interrogators would start interrogations at the same time as the Muslim call to prayers, renaming it a "call to interrogation."[81] During these interrogations, they reportedly built a religious shrine to Osama bin Laden and told the al-Qahtani, a Muslim, that he could only pray to bin Laden.[82] There are also examples of interrogators committing outrageous acts of disrespect towards a detainee's religious convictions as a method of interrogation. Al Darbi reported to CITF

[76] Ibid., 269.

[77] Ibid.

[78] Jane Mayer, *The Dark Side*, 207.

[79] Sworn Statement by a Detainee in *The Torture Papers: The Road to Abu Ghraib*, ed. Karen Greenberg and Joshua L. Dratel (New York: Caimbridge University Press, 2005), 524.

[80] Ibid.

[81] Derek S. Jeffreys, *Spirituality and the Ethics of Torture* (New York: Palgrave Macmillan, 2009), 37.

[82] Ibid.

investigators that an interrogator pulled out his penis, put it near al Darbi's face, and said, "This is your God."[83]

Combinations of Sleep Deprivation, Sensory Deprivation, and Physical Isolation

When several interrogation techniques were combined and used over an extended time period, the totality of their force on a detainee's mind appears to have multiplied the effect that each technique would have had on the detainees mind if it had been applied in isolation from the other techniques. This was illustrated in the case of al-Qahtani. The combined use of sleep deprivation, sensory deprivation, and physical isolation from other detainees for 48 of 54 days had the cumulative effect of driving Slahi into madness as he was observed crouching in the corner while talking to people who were not there.[84]

Denial of Human Dignity

There are also numerous examples of interrogators treating detainees like animals instead of humans. The U.S. Army's Schmidt-Furlow investigation found that Slahi's interrogators were permitted to make him wear a leash, to lead him around on a leash, and to make him do dog tricks.[85] Al-Qahtani's interrogators also put a leash on him and forced him to perform dog tricks.[86] A psychologist reportedly advised the CIA to put Abu Zubayda into a cage and treat him like an animal.[87]

[83] Bravin, *Terror Courts*, 269.

[84] Woodward, "Detainee Tortured, Says U.S. Official."

[85] Schmidt and Furlow, "Investigation into FBI Allegations of Detainee Abuse at Guantanamo Bay, Cuba Detention Facility," 19–20.

[86] Woodward, "Detainee Tortured, Says U.S. Official."

[87] Derek S. Jeffreys, *Spirituality and the Ethics of Torture* (New York: Palgrave Macmillan, 2009), 74.

The Gloves Came Off

In December 2002, the head of the CIA Counterterrorist Center, Cofer Black, testified to the House and Senate Intelligence Committees, "All I want to say is that there was 'before' 9/11 and 'after' 9/11. After 9/11 the gloves come off."[88] The phrase about the gloves coming off permeated U.S. culture, and it came to mean that the rules had changed. But nowhere did it resonate more than in the military and intelligence communities. This was exemplified by the August 2003 e-mail from a military intelligence officer in the Army's Fourth Infantry Division. The e-mail tasked other officers to meet with interrogators and to provide the intelligence officer with an interrogation techniques "wish list."[89] The intelligence officer explained:

> The gloves are coming off gentlemen regarding these detainees, [name redacted] has made it clear that we want these individuals broken. Casualties are mounting and we need to start gathering info to help protect our fellow soldiers from any further attacks.[90]

Many who responded to the e-mail concurred in the sentiment that restrictions on interrogation techniques had a negative impact on intelligence collection; however, one person's theology and professional military education in the just war tradition was robust enough to recognize that there were deeper theological and professional values that were more valuable than security. He responded:

[88] Dana Priest and Barton Gellman, "U.S. Decries Abuse but Defends Interrogations" *Washington Post*, Dec 26, 2002.

[89] Redacted Name, E-mail from an Army Officer in Fourth Infantry Division, Aug. 14, 2003, http://nsarchive.gwu.edu/torturingdemocracy/documents/20030814.pdf.

[90] Ibid.

> As for "the gloves need to come off . . ." we need to take a deep breath and remember who we are. Those gloves are most definitely NOT based on Cold War or WWII enemies—they are based on clearly established standards of international law to which we are signatories and in part the originators. Those in turn derive from practices commonly accepted as morally correct . . . . It comes down to standards of right and wrong—something we cannot just put aside when we find it inconvenient . . . . BOTTOM LINE: We are American soldiers, heirs of a long tradition of staying on the high ground. We need to stay there.[91]

At the bottom of the e-mail, the author placed a citation to Psalm 24:3–8. The author appears to be pointing his readers towards the just war tradition of warriors like King David and the Christ that David wrote about. The passage provides

> Who shall ascend the hill of the LORD? And who shall stand in his holy place? He who has clean hands and a pure heart, who does not lift up his soul to what is false and does not swear deceitfully. He will receive blessing from the LORD and righteousness from the God of his salvation. Such is the generation of those who seek him, who seek the face of the God of Jacob. Selah. Lift up your heads, O gates! And be lifted up, O ancient doors, that the King of glory may come in. Who is this King of glory? The LORD, strong and mighty, the LORD, mighty in battle![92]

What happens when the law creates a vacuum of authority? John Calvin's teaching on the second use of the law should have led Christians serving in positions of national security to understand that

[91] Ibid.
[92] Ps. 24:3–8.

a decision to remove Common Article 3's application to detainees would foreseeably lead others to give in to the temptation to mistreat detainees. In his *Institutes of the Christian Religion*, Calvin taught that the three uses of law are (1) to expose a person's unrighteous conduct,[93] (2) to restrain evil and misconduct,[94] and (3) to reveal what is pleasing to God.[95] When President Bush removed Common Article 3 as a restraint on the treatment of detainees, it was easier for persons in government to approve the use of pain, sexual exploitation, religious exploitation, the conditions that diminish the detainee's ability to reason, and dehumanization as interrogation techniques. It was equally foreseeable that the approval of those techniques would have a waterfall effect in which the unapproved use of these techniques would become widespread, leading to the abuse of detainees at the Bagram detention center in Afghanistan, the Abu Ghraib facility in Iraq, and at the Guantanamo Bay facility in Cuba.

The question is: when the law is removed as a restraint on the treatment of enemy detainees, can Scripture and the just war tradition fill the vacuum? For some Christians, their theology was not strong enough to fill the vacuum. Army Specialist Charles A. Graner, who was one of several soldiers court-martialed for the mistreatment of detainees at Abu Ghraib, showed a friend a digital picture of naked detainees and said, "The Christian in me says it's wrong," but that the corrections officer in him enjoyed it.[96] Graner knew enough to

[93] John Calvin, *Institutes of the Christian Religion*, trans. Henry Beveridge (Grand Rapids: Wm. B. Eerdmans, 1989) 2.7.6.

[94] Ibid., 2.7.10.

[95] Ibid., 2.7.12–13.

[96] Kate Zernike, "The Reach of War: The Witnesses; Only a Few Spoke Up on Abuse As Many Soldiers Stayed Quiet," *New York Times*, May 22, 2004, http://www.nytimes.com/2004/05/22/world/reach-war-witnesses-only-few-spoke-up-abuse-many-soldiers-stayed-silent.html. Episcopal Priest, Fleming Rutledge would later preach about Charles Graner's statement, "It seemed that he had two selves, the Christian self and the MP self, and the two selves were not speaking to one another." Fleming Rutledge, "Abu Ghraib and the Mind of the Trinity," June 6, 2003,

determine that the Bible prohibited Christians from engaging in the sexual exploitation of detainees among many other acts, but he enjoyed the control and domination of another human being. Other Christians, like LtCol Couch and the unnamed officer in the Fourth Infantry Division, had a theology and understanding of the just war tradition that led them to act on their convictions.

Conclusions on How the U.S. Treated Detainees

The purpose of this chapter was to establish a background on how the U.S. treated detainees before the following chapters analyze whether that treatment is biblically objectionable. This chapter demonstrated that when President Bush removed the law restraining the treatment of detainees and made military necessity the paramount priority for the state, the U.S. approved new interrogation techniques that fell into the following categories: (1) pain and physical abuse, (2) sexual exploitation, (3) religious exploitation, (4) assaults on reason using sensory deprivation, sleep deprivation and isolation and (5) the treatment of detainees like animals. This chapter also raised the issue of what will fill the vacuum when the law is removed and only replaced with a policy. This chapter demonstrated that the removal of Common Article 3 resulted, directly and indirectly, in the pictures at Abu Ghraib and the administration's admission that al-Qahtani was tortured. The following chapters will explore the just war tradition and the biblical doctrines that it rests upon, and argue that Christians should object to the use of pain, sexual exploitation, religious exploitation, and a denial of the detainee's humanity as interrogation techniques.

---

http://www.generousorthodoxy.org/sermons/abu-ghraib-and-the-mind-of-the-trinity.aspx.

2

Overview of the Just War Tradition

Christian love does not simply hover over the realities of political life. . . . It incarnates itself in the actualities and provides itself grounds for action by fashioning discriminating judgments between acts of war proposed to be put forth.[1]

The just war tradition is the theological, philosophical, and ethical middle ground between realism and pacifism. Realism assumes that unlimited war may be legitimate while pacifism believes that no war is legitimate. Alternatively, the just war tradition argues that Christ's teaching on love[2] provides the twin-born justification and limitation on war.[3] The Christian's love of neighbor compels the Christian to fight sacrificially to defend them against aggression and injustice while surrounding noncombatants with immunity from intentional harm.

The just war tradition began with Augustine reacting to the pacifist teachings of other Patristics and arguing that Christians could be soldiers.[4] Aquinas continued to develop the tradition, as did Calvin

[1] Paul Ramsey, *The Just War: Force and Political Responsibility* (Lanham, MD: Rowman & Littlefield Publishers, Inc., 2002), 164.

[2] Luke 10:25–37; Matt. 5:43–45; Matt. 25:31–46.

[3] Ramsey, *The Just War*, 144.

[4] David D. Corey and J. Daryl Charles, *The Just War Tradition* (Wilmington, DE: Intercollegiate Studies Institute, 2012), 56.

as he reacted to pacifist Anabaptist teachings.[5] It was during the fifteenth century that lawyers such as Grotius started to join the tradition to fashion the first conceptions of a law of war.[6] Then the just war tradition's beliefs in love and justice as warrants and limitations on warfare gave way as the world turned to the realism exemplified by Clausewitz and the view of war as merely a continuation of politics by other means.[7] However, during the twentieth century, the just war tradition became resurgent in reaction to the indiscriminate killing of civilian noncombatants during World Wars I and II, the threat of nuclear annihilation during the Cold War, and the threat to civilians posed by the war of counter-insurgency in Vietnam. Just war scholars such as James Turner Johnson challenged Christian pacifists to see that the Bible was not a presumption against war but a presumption against injustice,[8] and Paul Ramsey challenged Christian realists such as Reinhold Niebuhr for failing to recognize that love provides a justification for war and the killing of combatants while also providing a limitation on war that protects noncombatants.[9]

Content and History of the Just War Tradition

The just war tradition is divided into two distinct branches: *jus ad bellum* and *jus in bello*.[10] *Jus ad bellum* considers the justification to

[5] Keith Pavlischek, "Reinhold Niebuhr, Christian Realism, and Just War Theory: A Critique," in *Christianity and Power Politics Today*, ed. Eric Patterson (New York: Palgrave Macmillan, 2008), 54.

[6] International and Operational Law Department, *The Law of War Deskbook* (Charlottesville, VA: U.S. Army Judge Advocate General's Legal Center and School, 2004), 12.

[7] Carl von Clausewitz, *On War*, trans. J.J. Graham, vol. 3, (London: Kegan, Trench, Trubner & Co 1908), 121.

[8] James Turner Johnson, "The Broken Tradition," *National Interest* 45 (Fall 1996): 27–36.

[9] Pavlischek, "Reinhold Niebuhr, Christian Realism, and Just War Theory: A Critique," 61.

[10] This paper acknowledges the developing doctrine of *jus post bellum* as too nascent and beyond the scope of this paper to justify a worthy discussion.

go to war while *jus in bello* considers the limitations on conducting it. *Jus ad bellum* provides a framework composed of international law, biblical doctrines, and ethical concerns that inform state leaders considering whether the state may justly go to war, while *jus in bello* is the branch that informs leaders, commanders, and soldiers on the justice of their methods for fighting the war after the state has decided to engage in it. For example, the *jus ad bellum* framework for analyzing whether the resort to war is just or moral asks the following questions: (1) will the war be fought for a just cause, (2) has a legitimate authority made the decision for war, (3) will the war be fought with a right intention, (4) is the resort to war the last resort, (5) is the good to be achieved by the war proportional against the harm that will be caused by war, and (6) is the overall goal of the war to achieve a more secure peace than the peace that existed before the war?[11] In contrast, *jus in bello* is not concerned with whether the war was begun for just reasons but whether the war is being fought with just methods.

The *jus in bello* framework has two principles: (1) discrimination and (2) proportionality.[12] First, discrimination asks whether the methods of fighting discriminate between combatants and noncombatants. For example, is the harm only intentionally targeting military objectives (e.g., soldiers, military bases, and military equipment) of the

---

Suffice it to say that *jus post bellum* (justice after war) guides the victorious nation in conducting a just occupation after the conclusion of hostilities, engaging in political restructuring of the aggressive country in such a way that will lead to a lasting peace, holding war criminals accountable, and extracting reparations. See, e.g., Richard P. DiMeglio, "The Evolution of the Just War Tradition: Defining *Jus Post Bellum*" *Military Law Review* 186 (2006): 116–63.

[11] James Turner Johnson, *Can Modern War Be Just?* (New Haven: Yale University Press, 1984), 3.

[12] James Turner Johnson, *Ideology, Reason, and the Limitation of War* (Princeton, New Jersey: Princeton University Press, 1999), 18; William V. O'Brien, *The Conduct of Just and Limited War* (New York: Praeger Publishers, 1981), 37.

aggressor nation while avoiding the intentional targeting of non-military targets (e.g., civilians, prisoners, elementary schools, and churches)? This principle stands for the doctrine of noncombatant immunity, which prohibits the intentional harming of noncombatants.

Second, proportionality asks whether the military method of warfare is proportional to the military or political end being pursued.[13] While the traditional measure of proportionality engages in something akin to a balancing test, some methods of warfare have been judged so morally repugnant[14] that it has been deemed *mala in se* (i.e., methods morally wrong in themselves).[15] Such methods would never be proportional to any end being pursued.[16] For example, the prohibitions in international law against genocide, against the use of rape as a method of warfare,[17] and the traditional just war view of torture[18] are several of the many examples of means that have been determined to be morally wrong in every situation.

The Rise and Demise of the Just War Tradition

The Patristics used Scripture to find just war positions. Initially, many of the early church fathers such as Tertullian[19] (160–225 A.D.) and Origen[20] (184–253 A.D.) argued that the teachings of Scripture

[13] O'Brien, *The Conduct of Just and Limited War*, 37.

[14] James Turner Johnson, "Torture: A Just War Perspective," *The Review of Faith & International Affairs* 5, 2 (2007): 31.

[15] Brian Orend, *The Morality of Warfare* (Toronto: Broadview Press, 2006), 123.

[16] James Turner Johnson, *Morality and Contemporary Warfare* (New Haven: Yale University Press, 1999), 29.

[17] Orend, *The Morality of War*, 123.

[18] Johnson, "Torture: A Just War Perspective," 31; Orend, *The Morality of War*, 123.

[19] In Chapter 11 of *De Corona*, Tertullian made his objection to Christian military service based upon idolatry and the "quasi-religious" nature of Roman military service at the time. Corey and Charles, *The Just War Tradition*, 31.

[20] In *Contra Celsus*, Origen argued that the teachings of Christ against

prohibited Christian military service. They based their pacifist views on the teachings of Jesus in the Sermon on the Mount, which they believed to require non-violent peacemaking (Matthew 5:9), to prohibit retaliation such as an eye for an eye (Matthew 5:38), and to require the Christian to turn the other cheek (Matthew 5:39). Augustine (354–430) responded to such arguments by showing that Scripture did not prohibit military service since David, in the Old Testament, engaged in military service and Christ, in the New Testament, found the Roman centurion to be more faithful than all of Israel in Matthew 8:8–10.[21] In reviewing the Sermon on the Mount, Augustine did not find a prohibition against war in Christ's blessing of the peacemakers; rather, he finds Christ making peace to be an end that in some cases can only be procured through war against those who would attack the Christian.[22] The influence of Augustine upon later just war writers made him the father of the just war tradition.[23]

During the Middle Ages, the just war tradition evolved under Thomas Aquinas (1225–74) and the scholastics to include non-religious sources such as the code of chivalry.[24] Aquinas developed a juristic model to guide Christian rulers in deciding when they were justified in going to war.[25] In his *Summa Theologica*, Aquinas found three conditions necessary for a just war: (1) the decision of a legitimate authority such as a sovereign to engage in war, (2) a just cause (e.g., to establish peace) and (3) a right intention.[26]

---

vengeance and the teachings of Paul to put on the whole armor of God required Christians to act as spiritual intercessors for the state rather than material defenders of the state. Ibid., 35.

[21] Ibid., 57 (citing Augustine's *Letter 189 to Boniface*).

[22] Ibid.

[23] Ibid., 53.

[24] O'Brien, *The Conduct of Just and Limited War*, 13.

[25] International and Operational Law Department, *The Law of War Deskbook* (Charlottesville, VA: U.S. Army Judge Advocate General's Legal Center and School, 2004), 12.

[26] Corey and Charles, *The Just War Tradition*, 78–79.

During the enlightenment, Reformers such as Martin Luther (1483–1546) and John Calvin (1509–64) maintained the Augustinian just war view. Then Hugo Grotius (1583–1645), writing *On the Law of War and Peace*, argued for just war principles to be rooted in law rather than religion.[27] Theologians such as Luther and Calvin continued to develop just war positions as part of their theology on the relationship between church and state;[28] however, lawyers abandoned the theological basis for the law of war as they developed a new basis upon (1) the customs and practices that nations appeared to follow out of obligation and (2) written treaties and conventions negotiated by states (e.g., the Hague Treaties, Geneva Conventions, and the U.N. Charter among others). At the same time as the ascendancy of jurisprudence as an authority over theology in international relations, the just war era came to an end and the "war as fact" period began. Peacemaking through justice was replaced by realism and its belief that the sovereign interests of each state should be the paramount rationale guiding decisions on when to wage war and how to wage war.

Christian Realism and Reinhold Niebuhr

Though he is not a just war proponent, Reinhold Niebuhr bears mentioning due to his prominence as a Protestant theologian, Christian realist, and strong defender of democracy against Soviet communism during the warfare of the twentieth century.[29] While secular realism accepts war as the way of the world in which states act out of their own interests, Niebuhr had a "keen awareness" of human sin and oppression combined with an appreciation for the role of coercion in maintaining and protecting just, democratic civilization.[30] While Niebuhr provided a philosophical basis for Christians to participate in

[27] International and Operational Law Department, *The Law of War Deskbook*, 12.

[28] Corey and Charles, *The Just War Tradition*, 85–128.

[29] Ibid., 208.

[30] Ibid., 211–12.

war, he did not articulate a Scriptural justification[31] the way that Augustine, Aquinas, and Calvin found justification in Christ's teaching on love and Paul's teaching on justice in Romans 13:3–4. Instead, Niebuhr understood the "ethic of Jesus" in the same way that pacifists did and believed that adherence to it would be "disastrous for sociopolitical life" if followed without "consideration of the consequences."[32] Accordingly, theologians reasserted the just war tradition during the twentieth century as a reaction to the failure of Christian realism to provide a moral limitation on warfare.[33]

The Sources of Modern Just War Tradition

And so the atrocities of total war against noncombatants during the two World Wars[34] and the threat to civilians from nuclear weapons during the cold war[35] caused some scholars and theologians to return to the moral teachings of the just war tradition and the protections that *jus in bello* afforded. These moral restraints on the methods of warfare are now found in a plethora of authorities such as international law, Scripture, and the professional military ethics of soldiers, depending on the emphasis of the scholar. The following four perspectives are provided.

William V. O'Brien's Roman Catholic Perspective

William V. O'Brien, a Roman Catholic professor of government at Georgetown University, described just war tradition as a combination of positive law and natural law.[36] In his book, *The Just Conduct of*

[31] Ibid., 212.

[32] Reinhold Niebuhr, *An Interpretation of Christian Ethics* (New York: Harper & Brothers, 1935) 35–62.

[33] Pavlischek, "Reinhold Niebuhr, Christian Realism, and Just War Theory: A Critique," 61.

[34] O'Brien, *The Conduct of Just and Limited War*, 4.

[35] Johnson, *Morality and Contemporary Warfare*, 1, 3, 22; O'Brien, *The Conduct of Just and Limited War*, 365n12.

[36] O'Brien, *The Just Conduct of War*, 15.

War, O'Brien's priority was on the law as found in law of war authorities such as the Geneva Conventions of 1949. Natural law provided the general philosophical and moral rationale for the more specific international law. O'Brien found natural law in the historical just war tradition of Aquinas and the scholastics as viewed through the contemporary "social teaching of the Catholic Church" and the "scholarship of Protestant and secular moralists and philosophers."[37] However, O'Brien's reliance on Aquinas and the scholastics was not for their theology that interpreted Scripture but as an authoritative tradition among other authorities. He was dismissive of those in the Roman Catholic Church, particularly those arguing pacifist positions, who claimed a theological source in the teachings of Christ.[38]

Paul Ramsey's and Daryl Charles' Protestant Perspectives

Princeton University theologian Paul Ramsey, during the cold war, and Calvinist theologian J. Daryl Charles, during the twenty-first century wars in Iraq and Afghanistan, returned not only to the ideas of Augustine, Aquinas, and Calvin but to the practice of basing ideas in Scripture. Ramsey and Charles apply Scriptural ideas to the debates of their day: Ramsey with regard to nuclear war and the Vietnam War and Charles with regard to fighting terrorism. Ramsey and Charles concur with Augustine in finding that the primary origin of just war tradition is in the Christian love of neighbor[39] rather than abstract ideas such as natural law. On Jesus' teaching of the lawyer on the Good Samaritan,[40] Ramsey argued:

[37] Ibid., 4.

[38] Ibid., 15. This dismissiveness appears to be directed towards the U.S. Catholic Bishops 1983 pastoral letter on war and peace, which O'Brien and many other just war scholars including Paul Ramsey, James Turner Johnson, and J. Daryl Charles criticized as making a pacifist interpretation of the teachings of Christ in the sermon on the mount, which was contrary to the just war tradition of Augustine and Aquinas.

[39] Ramsey, *The Just War*, 142.

[40] Luke 10:25–37.

> It was an act of Christian love for the Good Samaritan to give help to the man who fell among thieves. But one step more, it may have been a work of charity for the inn-keeper to hold himself ready to receive beaten and wounded men, and for him to have conducted business so that he was solvent enough to extend credit to the Good Samaritan. By another step it would have been a work of charity, and not justice alone, to maintain and serve in a police patrol on the Jericho road to prevent such things from happening. By yet another step, it might well be a work of charity to resist, by force of arms, any external aggression against the social order that maintains police patrol along the road to Jericho. This means that, where the enforcement of an ordered community is not effectively present, it may be a work of justice and a work of charity to resort to other available and effective means of resisting injustice: what do you think Jesus would have made the Samaritan do if he had come upon the scene while the robbers were still at their fell work?[41]

Ramsey argues that these were the implications of neighbor-love that many Christians drew from the parable as they desired to "have the will of God reign and God's mercy shed" through their lives.[42] This is also the worldview that they carried with them as they engaged, appropriated, and refined Stoic concepts of natural justice.[43]

Ramsey also examined Jesus' Sermon on the Mount, which is the frequent foundation for pacifist arguments, but Ramsey saw different implications for neighbor-love. Admitting that Jesus taught his disciples that they should turn their other cheek, Ramsey argued that "he did not enjoin that his disciples should lift up the face of another

[41] Ramsey, *The Just War*, 142–43.
[42] Ibid., 143.
[43] Ibid.

oppressed man for *him* to be struck again on *his* other cheek."[44] In effect, Ramsey reasoned that a person may choose not to defend himself against oppression, but that is a personal decision that is appropriate when "one's own good's and life are alone at stake."[45] Neighbor-love ought to drive the Christian to act differently when his neighbor is being oppressed. Ramsey argued that people in a position to defend and protect their neighbors from oppression are required by neighbor-love to act, reasoning that "it is the work of love and mercy to deliver" a neighbor from tyranny and to protect them from oppression.[46]

Ramsey's argument that neighbor-love provides a *jus ad bellum* justification for a Christian's resort to force also provides a *jus in bello* justification for the principles of discrimination and proportionality. With regard to discrimination (i.e., the prohibition against direct attack on noncombatants), the neighbor-love that justifies killing the aggressive enemy would never justify the intentional harming of noncombatants as a means of getting to the enemy.[47] The love that makes aggressors the object of legitimate attack surrounds noncombatants with immunity from direct attack.[48] With regard to proportionality (i.e., the requirement that the method of warfare be proportionate to the political end sought), love for an immediate neighbor will suffer and allow some measure of indirect harm to the noncombatants who are the enemy's immediate neighbors so long as the harm is proportionate and not excessive in comparison to the military advantage to be gained from the direct attack upon the enemy combatant. In practical terms, the Christian's love for his immediate neighbors and countrymen that legitimizes his use of force in their defense also extends to his enemy's immediate neighbors and countrymen and de-legitimizes uses of force that would directly harm them

[44] Matt. 5:38–39.
[45] Ramsey, *The Just War*, 151.
[46] Ibid., 143.
[47] Ibid.
[48] Ibid., 151.

(i.e., the principle of discrimination) or would cause excessive indirect harm to them (i.e., the principle of proportionality).

Based upon the teachings of Christ and the theological implications that early Christians like Augustine drew from them, Ramsey argued how they should shape a Christian's conscience in the twentieth century. The implication for *jus ad bellum* issues is that nations and Christians serving as military personnel must sometimes engage in warfare to protect their neighbors and repress the bearer of aggressive hostile force.[49] However, the same neighbor-love that provides "legitimacy for the use of military force" also requires limits upon its use against other neighbors on the battlefield who are not participating in combat (e.g., noncombatants). As such, neighbor-love provides much of the Scriptural basis for the *jus in bello* principles that limit the conduct of war.

The Professional Military Ethicist's Perspective

U.S. Army Colonel Anthony Hartle, a professor of philosophy and military ethics at the United States Military Academy (West Point), draws clear connection between broad moral principles and the specific regulations in the law of war (e.g., the Geneva Conventions). For Colonel Hartle, those moral principles govern "military professionals" in the same way that professions like medicine and law are governed by principles.[50] The primary principle that Col Hartle discerned is that individual persons deserve respect as humans.[51] Colonel Hartle sees this principle embodied in the Geneva conventions requirement that military forces care for the sick and wounded,[52] care for the shipwrecked,[53] respect and protect prisoners of war[54] and

[49] Ibid., 143, 144–45.

[50] Anthony E. Hartle, *Moral Issues in Military Decision Making* (Lawrence, KS: University Press of Kansas, 2004), 71.

[51] Ibid.

[52] The First Geneva Convention For the Amelioration of the Condition of the Wounded and Sick.

[53] The Second Geneva Convention For the Amelioration of the Condition

the civilian population,[55] as well as the safeguards for noncombatants "from torture or cruel and inhuman punishment."[56] In those international laws, Hartle sees a requirement to honor the human dignity of persons who fit into these categories of those no longer participating in combat.[57]

For Colonel Hartle, this principle of human dignity is deontological and requires that it be followed without regard to the consequences.[58] This was demonstrated by conduct of the four Navy SEALs in the 2014 movie, *Lone Survivor*. The SEALs were trying to secretly infiltrate a village to kill a Taliban leader when they were inadvertently stumbled upon by two Afghan men and a young boy.[59] The Navy SEALs debated whether to kill them or release them and risk the Taliban being alerted. Navy SEAL Michael Luttrell provides the account that the SEALs voted to release the Afghans despite their suspicions that the Afghans would inform the Taliban of the SEAL's location. Soon after the release, the SEALs were overwhelmed by Taliban fighters, and three of the four SEALs were killed during a heroic battle in which three would win the Navy Cross and one would win the Medal of Honor.[60] Luttrell admits being tempted to kill the three civilian noncombatants, but he reports that he did not because, he said, "I am not a murderer."[61] The episode illustrates the deontological nature of the principles of discrimination in that military necessity (e.g., maintaining concealment of the SEAL team so that

---

of the Wounded, Sick and Shipwrecked.

[54] The Third Geneva Convention Relative to the Treatment of Prisoners of War.

[55] The Fourth Geneva Convention Relative to the Protection of Civilian Persons in Time of War.

[56] Hartle, *Moral Issues in Military Decision Making*, 72.

[57] Ibid., 72–73.

[58] Ibid., 77.

[59] Laura Blumenfeld, "The Sole Survivor," *Washington Post*, June 11, 2007, A1.

[60] Ibid.

[61] Ibid.

the mission may be completed) cannot justify harming civilian noncombatants.

The Philosophers' Perspectives

Michael Walzer, James Turner Johnson, and Jean Bethke Elshtain argue for the relevance of the just war tradition as historic ideas that should be applied to contemporary warfare. They observe the bankruptcy of realism in addressing the unavoidable human desire for morality in warfare. They argue for a return to the just war tradition as the historic, cultural framework upon which to base the public discourse on war. Walzer makes this argument based upon the historical evidence of a concern for morality during war.[62] While Walzer characterizes just war tradition as general morality, Johnson is more intentional in drawing upon Augustine and Christian sources of the moral wisdom found in "Western ideals, institutions, and experiences."[63] In addition to the religious sources, Johnson also finds that the just war tradition can be found in the law of war and military professional manuals.[64] Johnson's strength is as a scholar in reaching back and recovering the ideas of Augustine and Aquinas and showing how they are relevant and helpful when applied to modern issues and concerns—even torture.[65]

Conclusion

This chapter has argued that the just war tradition has always occupied the ethical middle ground between pacifism and realism. Christ's teaching on love provides the twin-born justification and limitation regarding war.[66] The neighbor-love in the *jus ad bellum*

[62] Michael Walzer, *Just and Unjust Wars* (New York: Perseus Books Group, 2006), 15.

[63] Johnson, *Morality and Contemporary Warfare*, 22.

[64] Ibid., 24.

[65] Ibid., 31.

[66] Ramsey, *The Just War*, 144.

branch rejects the pacifist position that would lead to the oppression of neighbors by aggressor nations, and the neighbor-love in the *jus in bello* branch rejects realism's failure to place limits on the methods of warfare that lead to the disproportionate harm of noncombatants.

The following chapters will examine the substance of the *jus in bello* branch and apply it to the methods of detainee treatment that were either officially approved by President Bush's administration or unofficially practiced by service members and members of the CIA. Chapter 3 will examine the *jus in bello* principles of discrimination, founded upon neighbor-love[67] and enemy-love,[68] and argue that detainees have always been considered noncombatants who must be protected by their captors from harm. Chapter 4 will examine the *jus in bello* principle of proportionality and argue that torture and cruel treatment is *mala in se* and can never be deemed proportional to the ends sought if they dehumanize and attack the *Imago Dei* in the detainee. Chapter 5 will examine the issue of dirty hands and argue that the just war tradition should reject dirty hands as a violation of discrimination's deontological character in the historic just war tradition. Finally, chapter 6 will examine the argument that Scripture gives Christians a warrant to harm detainees with clean hands, yet the chapter will demonstrate that those positions fail to reconcile their passages emphasizing justice with other passages emphasizing love.

[67] Luke 10:25–37.
[68] Matt. 5:43–45.

3

Discriminating Between Combatants and Noncombatants

And the King will answer them, 'Truly, I say to you, as you did it to one of the least of these my brothers, you did it to me.' . . . For I was hungry and you gave me no food, I was thirsty and you gave me no drink, I was a stranger and you did not welcome me, naked and you did not clothe me, sick and in prison and you did not visit me.'[1]

Discrimination is the first of the two jus in bello principles.[2] It asks whether a method of warfare distinguishes between targeting combatants and noncombatants with harm. To employ this principal, the combatant must determine the status of everyone he encounters on the battlefield and then treat that person accordingly. The just war tradition has always composed lists of persons who do not take a direct part in warfare and prohibited combatants from intentionally harming them.[3] During ancient times, the first lists included traditional categories of persons who do not take part in warfare: women, children, the aged and infirm, clergy and monks, peasants working in

[1] Matt. 25:40–43.

[2] James Turner Johnson, *Ideology, Reason, and the Limitation of War* (Princeton, NJ: Princeton University Press, 1999), 18; William V. O'Brien, *The Conduct of Just and Limited War* (New York: Praeger Publishers, 1981), 37.

[3] James Turner Johnson, "Torture: A Just War Perspective," *The Review of Faith & International Affairs* 5, 2 (2007): 31.

the fields, merchants, pilgrims, and ordinary townspeople.[4] During the later Middle Ages, the list was expanded to include combatants who could no longer fight because they were either wounded or captured.[5]

Today's formulation is found in the Geneva Conventions of 1949. The term combatants includes both (1) privileged belligerents who qualify for Prisoner of War (POW) status such as members of the armed forces and militias belonging to a state[6] and (2) unprivileged belligerents who fight and take a direct part in hostilities but are not part of an armed force or militia belonging to a state.[7] The term noncombatant essentially includes everyone else on the battlefield who is not taking a direct part in hostilities. During international armed conflict between two or more states, the common categories of

[4] Ibid.

[5] Ibid.

[6] Article 4 of the Third Geneva Convention uses "prisoners of war" as a term of art that specifically includes persons who were "Members of the armed forces of a Party to the conflict" as well as members of organized militias that fulfill the conditions of formality recognized by regular armed forces such as the following:

a) that of being commanded by a person responsible for his subordinates;
b) that of having a fixed distinctive sign recognizable at a distance;
c) that of carrying arms openly;
d) that of conducting their operations in accordance with the laws and customs of war.

This definition would not apply to Al Qaeda and Taliban detainees since they were not members of an armed force that was a party to the conflict or members of an organized militia with the four conditions. Accordingly, they are considered detainees who are entitled to humane treatment but not POWs who would have been entitled to all the protections of the Third Geneva Convention. Deputy Secretary of Defense, "DoD Detainee Program," (Washington, DC: Department of Defense, 2014).

[7] This paper excludes consideration of the *levee en masse*, a third category of Article 4 combatants who are those inhabitants of a territory that spontaneously rise up and take arms to resist invading forces. They are excluded because they have not been relevant during the Wars in Afghanistan and Iraq, which places them beyond the scope of this paper focused on detainee treatment during 2002–6.

noncombatants include (1) civilians;[8] (2) sick and wounded combatants[9] as well as those who are shipwrecked[10] and considered *hors de combat*,[11] POWs;[12] and unprivileged belligerents who are sick and wounded or detained.[13]

How shall combatants treat combatants? The section "Justification for Fighting Combatants" will demonstrate that when a combatant encounters an enemy combatant whose aim is to kill and oppress the combatant and his neighbor, the combatant's love for his neighbor requires him to oppose his enemy in order to return the world to a just peace.[14] Under this principle of combatant immunity, the Christian combatant is immune from prosecution for actions that would be common law crimes (e.g., murder or assault) if they were committed anywhere else in the world except that in this case they were committed on the battlefield against another combatant. The combatant's act of killing another combatant is not morally wrong but praiseworthy.[15]

[8] The Fourth Geneva Convention Relative to the Protection of Civilian Persons in Time of War.

[9] The First Geneva Convention For the Amelioration of the Condition of the Wounded and Sick.

[10] The Second Geneva Convention For the Amelioration of the Condition of the Wounded, Sick and Shipwrecked.

[11] Article 41 of Additional Protocol I to the Geneva Conventions provides the criteria that a person is *hors de combat* if (a) he is in the power of an adverse Party; (b) he clearly expresses an intention to surrender; or (c) he has been rendered unconscious or is otherwise incapacitated by wounds or sickness, and therefore is incapable of defending himself; provided that in any of these cases he abstains from any hostile act and does not attempt to escape.

[12] The Third Geneva Convention Relative to the Treatment of Prisoners of War.

[13] Common Article 3 of the Geneva Conventions of 1949.

[14] James Turner Johnson, *Can Modern War Be Just?* (New Haven, CT: Yale University Press, 1986), 3–4; Jean Bethke Elshtain, "Reflections on the Problem of 'Dirty Hands,'" in *Torture: A Collection*, ed. Sanford Levinson (Oxford: Oxford University Press, 2004), 81.

[15] Darrell Cole, "Torture and Just War," *Journal of Religious Ethics* 40, 1 (2012): 47.

How shall combatants treat noncombatants? The section "The Limitation from Harming Noncombatants" will demonstrate that the same biblical principle of neighbor-love that provided the justification to use force against aggressors also provides the limitation on the use of force against noncombatants, which includes former combatants whose aggression has ceased because he has been captured or become wounded or permanently returned to civilian life.[16] In a sense, the scope of neighbor-love expands to include the wounded or detained enemy. Neighbor-love expands to overlap the biblical teaching on enemy-love.[17] Both loves protect the wounded or detained enemy from abuse while held in the hands of his enemies.[18]

Justification for Fighting Combatants

The law of war implicitly permits the combatants of one state to use force against the combatants of another state when the states are in international armed conflict.[19] That rule has never been codified into international law and there has been very little scholarly treatment of it because it is simply recognized as a lawful custom and practice among states. In other words, that is what states pay their soldiers to do—kill the enemy.

While lawyers have not debated the authority of combatants to use force against each other, theologians and philosophers have. In finding the biblical middle ground between pacifism and realism, the just war tradition has generally determined that combatants may use force in defense of their state to kill the combatants of the aggressor state because (1) God has delegated the power of the sword to the

[16] Ramsey, *The Just War*, 144.

[17] Matt. 5:43–48; Luke 6:35–36; Rom. 12:20; Prov. 25:22.

[18] The Fourth Geneva Convention relative to the Protection of Civilian Persons in Time of War, Article 16.

[19] International and Operational Law Department, *The Law of War Deskbook* (Charlottesville, VA: U.S. Army Judge Advocate General's Legal Center and School, 2012), 138.

rulers of the state to carry out the wrath of God on the wrongdoer[20] and (2) Christians should wield the ruler's sword and defend the state because of their love for their neighbors[21] as well as out of a demand for justice against the aggressor.[22]

The State's Power of the Sword

In Romans 13:3–4, the Apostle Paul describes God's delegation of the power of the sword to rulers in order to punish wrongdoing. While this is commonly invoked as authority for the use of capital punishment within a state's criminal justice system,[23] just war theologians consider the passage also to provide rulers with the authority to conduct a just war against wrongdoing. John Calvin reasoned, "Natural equity and duty, therefore demand that princes be armed not only to repress private crimes by judicial inflictions, but to defend the subjects committed to their guardianship."[24] Calvin further explained, "Nay, if they justly punish those robbers . . . , will they allow the whole country to be robbed and devastated with impunity?"[25] However, rulers do not wield the sword by themselves against another state's armies. Rulers need soldiers to wield it for them.

Christians Should Wield the State's Sword

The Bible provides numerous examples of God's faithful men killing enemies during just wars. Abraham set out with 318 trained men on a "military expedition to rescue his nephew Lott"[26] who had been captured and carried off by the King of Elam, the King of

[20] Rom. 13:3–4, 1 Peter 2:13–17.

[21] Ramsey, *The Just War*, 143.

[22] John Murray, *Principles of Conduct: Aspects of Biblical Ethics* (Grand Rapids: Wm. B. Eerdmans, 1957), 179.

[23] John Jefferson Davis, *Evangelical Ethics* (Phillipsburg, NJ: P&R Publishing, 2004), 211.

[24] John Calvin, *Institutes of the Christian Religion* (Grand Rapids: Wm. B. Eerdmans, 1989), 4.20.11.

[25] Ibid.

[26] Davis, *Evangelical Ethics*, 248.

Goiim, the King of Shinar, and the King of Ellasar.[27] David is presented as faithful in killing tens of thousands of Philistines.[28] The inspired writers of the New Testament continued to praise King David and the Judges of Israel like Joshua as faithful men "who through faith conquered kingdoms, enforced justice . . . became mighty in war, [and] put foreign armies to flight."[29]

Just war theologians have also found support in the Gospels for faithful soldiering. Calvin found John the Baptist's instructions to the Roman soldiers in Luke 3:14 to be evidence in support of faithful soldiering.[30] John the Baptist had been preaching the message of repentance, and Roman soldiers responded by asking, "What shall we do?" John did not instruct them to throw down their weapons or to turn the other cheek.[31] Instead, he instructed them not to oppress out of self-interest (i.e., not to extort money but to be content in their wages).[32] In Acts 10, the Holy Spirit fell on the Roman centurion Cornelius while the Apostle Peter was preaching the Gospel, and Peter called for him to be baptized without ever telling Cornelius to leave military service. Similarly, Augustine found it noteworthy that Christ praised the Roman Centurion's faith and healed his daughter while never directing him to leave his position of authority in the Roman army.[33]

Consideration of all of these precedents of faithful military service in the Old and New Testaments raises the question of why they fought. Paul Ramsey and John Murray stand for the propositions that the Bible not only permits Christians to engage in war but that Scriptures instruct Christians to engage in just wars and serve as rulers

[27] Gen. 14:13–16.

[28] 1 Sam. 18:7.

[29] Heb. 11:33–34.

[30] Calvin, *Institutes*, 4.20.12.

[31] Corey and Charles, *The Just War Tradition*, 222–23.

[32] Luke 3:14.

[33] Corey and Charles, *The Just War Tradition*, 223 (citing Augustine, *Against Faustus the Manichean* 22.73–79).

or soldiers in order to (1) love their neighbors and (2) demand justice from aggressor states that do wrong.

Christian Neighbor-Love

As introduced in chapter 2, Princeton University theologian Paul Ramsey argued that people in a position to defend and protect their neighbors from oppression are required by neighbor-love to act, reasoning that "it is the work of love and mercy to deliver" a neighbor from tyranny and to protect them from oppression.[34] Ramsey based this on the implications from Jesus' parable of the Good Samaritan. Jesus taught that the Samaritan showed love for his victimized Jewish neighbor.[35] Ramsey asked what Jesus would have had the Samaritan do if he had arrived during the robbery and beating.[36] Ramsey believes that neighbor-love would have required the Samaritan to defend the victim against the attackers. Ramsey takes the implications further by arguing that neighbor-love could lead a Christian to police the Jericho road and to resist "armed aggression against the social order."[37] To do so would exemplify sacrificial love.

The Ruler's Demand for Justice

Princeton Seminary theologian John Murray argued that the soldier may reflect not only God's character of love but also his character for righteousness, holiness, and justice.[38] Based on Romans 13:3–4, Murray wrote like Calvin before him, "The wounding and killing involved [in war] are the use of the sword which God has put into the hands of the civil magistrate as the instrument of maintaining justice and punishing evil-doers."[39] Murray realistically admitted that most of the warfare that has been conducted throughout history has not been

[34] Ramsey, *The Just War*, 143.
[35] Luke 10:27–37.
[36] Ramsey, *The Just War*, 143.
[37] Ibid., 142.
[38] Murray, *Principles of Conduct*, 176.
[39] Ibid., 179.

righteous but "utterly contrary to the requirements of our Lord's teaching and are to be unsparingly denounced."[40] Standing on Christ's teaching to the lawyer in the verses preceding the Good Samaritan parable, Murray believed that love is "first of all love to God and therefore love of justice. Hence, when we view the demand of love and its broader proportions, the demand of love and the demand of justice are really one."[41] Yet, Murray cautioned Christians that this is narrow authority and that the sword should never be used out of vindictive revenge or malicious hate.[42] Murray reminded the Christian that the demand for justice is not incompatible with the Christ's requirement to love enemies.[43] This is the "paradox of love and wrath"[44] that God's character exhibits and that He calls upon his rulers and their soldiers to reflect in their characters.

The Limitation from Harming Noncombatants

Having considered the targeting of combatants in the previous section, this section considers the flip side of the principle of discrimination: the requirement to protect noncombatants from targeting and intentional harm. This section will consider noncombatants according to the following four categories: (1) civilians, (2) soldiers who become sick and wounded, (3) soldiers who are captured and become Prisoners of War, (4) unprivileged belligerents who are captured and become detainees because they do not meet the requirements to be categorized as Prisoners of Wars (e.g., al-Qaeda did not meet the requirements because they were a non-state group that did not fight as an armed force or militia belonging to a state). This book will refer to these detained unprivileged belligerents as "detainees."

[40] Ibid.
[41] Ibid.
[42] Ibid.
[43] Ibid.
[44] Davis, *Evangelical Ethics*, 251.

The first category of noncombatant (i.e., civilians) is the most classic example while the other three categories encompass former combatants who become *hors de combat*, out of combat, and are no longer in the fight.[45] The law of war requires that soldiers "respect (not attack) and protect (care for)" these former enemies.[46] The just war tradition provides theological rationale in that the ultimate goal of attacking combatants is not only to kill the combatant but to incapacitate or stop his combatancy.[47] Once his combatancy has ceased, and the enemy is defenseless in the hands of his captor, the Scriptural exhortations to Christians to love their enemies take on new importance.[48]

[45] Article 41 of Additional Protocol I to the Geneva Conventions provides the criteria that a person is *hors de combat* if (a) he is in the power of an adverse Party; (b) he clearly expresses an intention to surrender; or (c) he has been rendered unconscious or is otherwise incapacitated by wounds or sickness, and therefore is incapable of defending himself; provided that in any of these cases he abstains from any hostile act and does not attempt to escape.

[46] International and Operational Law Department, *The Law of War Deskbook* (Charlottesville: VA: U.S. Army Judge Advocate General's Legal Center and School, 2012), 138.

[47] Ramsey, *The Just War*, 509n3.

[48] It is on this point that evangelical professor Daniel Heimbach of Southeastern Baptist Seminary re-characterizes the principle of discrimination as something else. See Daniel Heimbach, "The Problem with Assessing Torture," *Global Journal of Classic Theology* 10, 1 (undated) http://www.globaljournalct.com/wp-content/uploads/2014/08/Daniel_Heimbach_Torture_vol_10_no_1.pdf. In his framework for considering whether to apply that he calls "coercive" and "regrettable forms of interrogation," he employs the *jus in bello* principle of Discrimination, stating that interrogators "must only use coercion with combatants." However, Heimbach makes the argument that coercive interrogation may be employed against some prisoners if they are "threatening national security and public safety." Heimbach's argument would have the effect of expanding the definition of combatant to include some prisoners, which is a break from the just war tradition. Heimbach is unwilling to see the person change in legal status and moral or ethical status from combatant to detainee. Heimbach is right to characterize interrogation as "itself a form of war," but the state should not be waging war against a restrained and defenseless prisoner. The

The Bible provides ample support for the just war tradition of respecting and protecting enemies who are no longer fighting. Jesus turned his world's conventional wisdom, on the treatment of enemies, upside down when he said:

> "You have heard that it was said, 'You shall love your neighbor and hate your enemy.' But I say to you, Love your enemies and pray for those who persecute you, so that you may be sons of your Father who is in heaven. For he makes his sun rise on the evil and on the good, and sends rain on the just and on the unjust. For if you love those who love you, what reward do you have?[49]

John Murray believes that Jesus is teaching his followers to treat their enemies the way God treats His enemies—with compassion.[50] The Apostle Paul reminded the Church in Rome that that they were the recipients of God's compassion on his enemies since they were once his enemies. Paul wrote, "For while we were enemies we were reconciled to God by the death of his Son."[51] God sacrificially loved his enemies. He gave his Son to die for them. Therefore, Christians should identify with a defenseless enemy and have compassion on him even if they have to act sacrificially.

The Apostle Paul gives practical examples of enemy-love as he expounds on Proverbs 25:22:

---

prisoner meet the definition of *hors de combat* in that he is "in the power of an adverse Party" as defined by Article 41 of Additional Protocol 1. Daniel R. Heimbach, "Daniel Heimbach on Torture," *First Things* (Jan. 6, 2010), http://www.firstthings.com/blogs/ firstthoughts/2010/01/daniel-heimbach-on-torture.

[49] Matt. 5:43–46.

[50] Murray, *Principles of Conduct*, 177–78.

[51] Rom. 5:10.

> Repay no one evil for evil, but give thought to do what is honorable in the sight of all. If possible, so far as it depends on you, live peaceably with all. Beloved, never avenge yourselves, but leave it to the wrath of God, for it is written, "Vengeance is mine, I will repay, says the Lord." To the contrary, "if your enemy is hungry, feed him; if he is thirsty, give him something to drink; for by so doing you will heap burning coals on his head." Do not be overcome by evil, but overcome evil with good.[52]

Here Paul makes three points that specifically apply to the circumstance of a Christian soldier who wounds or captures an enemy in one moment and then in the next moment is required by the law of war, Scripture, and morality to respect and protect that enemy. First, Paul's teaching should cause Christians not to take revenge on their enemy who may have been shooting at them or may have injured one of their fellow soldiers only moments before becoming *hors de combat*. Secondly, Paul's teaching provides Christians with imperatives to provide for the physical wellbeing of their enemies. But, thirdly, Paul provides the caveat "so far as it depends on you" that when applied to the combatant would mean that he is exempt from such requirements when his enemy continues to physically resist detention. Significant force may be necessary to detain the enemy but that force is for a lawfully permitted purpose that is a different purpose than interrogation.

Civilians

As discussed in the introduction to this chapter, the earliest lists of noncombatants included those persons (e.g., women, children, the aged and infirm, clergy and monks, peasants working their land, merchants, pilgrims, and ordinary townspeople) that the modern law of war considers civilians.[53] In the just war tradition, civilians are

[52] Rom. 12:17–21.

[53] Article 50 of First Additional Protocol to the Geneva Conventions of

referred to as innocents[54] because they cannot be guilty of the unjust war that their state and its soldiers are guilty of starting.[55] A counter-argument is that civilian populations are guilty because of their indirect involvement by financing the war with their taxes,[56] but this argument is not persuasive since taxes are mandatory in every state in the world and are coerced from the citizen[57] without regard for whether the citizen supports the war or not. Another counterargument is that the population of the enemy state has a shared interest and shared destiny with the leaders and soldiers fighting the war and that they should all be viewed as a whole, but this argument fails to provide a basis for the guilt of the infants and children who would surely become victims if the civilian population is targeted.[58] There are other arguments, but in the end, there is no justification for the intentional targeting of civilians that the just war tradition accepts as moral.

Terrorists like those on 9/11 are defined by the violation of the principle of discrimination because their focus is on targeting and killing innocent civilians. Daryl Charles provides a definition of a terrorist threat as "the deliberate and systematic murder, maiming,

---

1949 is the modern definition for civilian. Article 50 defines the term civilian to include everyone on the battlefield who does not belong to one of the groups of combatants in Article 4(a)(1), (2), (3), and (6) of the Third Geneva Conventions, which generally amounts to members of the armed forces and militias belonging to a state. The U.S. considers this definition to be part of customary international law binding on the United States. See W. Hays Parks, "1977 Protocols Additional to the Geneva Conventions: Customary International Law Implications" (May 9, 1986) in *Law of War Annual Documentary Supplement*, ed. J. Porter Harlow (Charlottesville, VA: U.S. Judge Advocate General's Legal Center and School, 2014).

[54] J. Daryl Charles, *Between Pacifism and Jihad: Just War and Christian Tradition* (Downer's Grove, IL: InterVarsity Press, 2005), 160.

[55] Ibid., 136.

[56] Brian Orend, *The Morality of Warfare* (Toronto: Broadview Press, 2006), 113.

[57] Ibid.

[58] Ibid.

and menacing of the innocent to inspire fear for political ends."[59] Charles points out that terrorists do not even have to kill many civilians to achieve their ends since a few well planned highly public murders of civilians will cause fear in the civilian population.[60] Khalid Sheik Mohammed's beheading of *Wall Street Journal* reporter Daniel Pearl[61] is an example of a single murder that continues to reverberate in the American population's memory many years later due to murder's senseless brutality and horror against an innocent journalist. Terrorists intentionally cross the line and break the *jus in bello* principle of discrimination because the breaking of that social norm is what creates the fear in the victimized population;[62] yet, that violation is what justifies the victimized state's just cause to go to war against the terrorist (e.g., the U.S. response to 9/11 in going to war against Afghanistan).

Soldiers Who Become Sick and Wounded

Soldiers should be discriminating in their treatment of sick and wounded enemies because the Bible calls upon Christians to show mercy to those who are sick. In Matthew 25, Jesus taught that the final judgment will include consideration of a person's acts of charity towards the least of Jesus' brothers who were sick.[63] In the context of the final judgment, the least of Jesus' brothers is specifically a reference to Christian believers,[64] but the act of charity towards Christians who are sick is representative of Christ's concern for all who are sick

[59] Charles, *Between Pacifism and Jihad*, 150.

[60] Ibid., 152.

[61] Peter Finn, "Khalid Sheik Mohammed killed U.S. journalist Daniel Pearl, report finds," *Washington Post*, Jan. 20, 2011, http://www.washingtonpost.com/wp-dyn/content/article/2011/01/20/AR2011012000057.html.

[62] Charles, *Between Pacifism and Jihad*, 153.

[63] Matt. 25:39–40.

[64] R.T. France, *The Gospel of Matthew*, (Grand Rapids: Eerdmans, 2007), 964; Donald A. Hagner, *Matthew 1–13* (Nashville, TN: Thomas Nelson, 1993), 744–45.

in other generalized contexts.[65] For example, in Galatians 6:10, Paul exhorts Christians to do good towards everyone while emphasizing the importance of showing charity towards those in the household of faith.

Christians can see Christ's compassion for the sick and wounded in the First and Second Geneva Conventions requirements that the sick, wounded, and shipwrecked be respected and protected.[66] There, all states in the world have agreed in Article 12 to care for the sick, wounded, and shipwrecked without any distinction or priority as to whether the sick and wounded person is from the same state or the enemy state. Article 12 states:

> They shall be treated humanely and cared for by the Party to the conflict in whose power they may be, without any adverse distinction founded on sex, race, nationality, religion, political opinions, or any other similar criteria. . . . Only urgent medical reasons [not nationality] will authorize priority in the order of treatment to be administered.[67]

The reciprocity expected between states—to treat each other's wounded as they would their own—reflects the Bible's requirement for Christians to love their neighbors as themselves[68] and to love their

[65] John Calvin, *Commentary on a Harmony of the Evangelists*, vol. 3 (Grand Rapids: Baker Books, 2005), 181. There Calvin provides, "Believers only are expressly recommended to our notice; not that he bids us altogether despise others, but because the more nearly a man approaches to God, he ought to be more highly esteemed by us; for though there is a common tie that tie that binds all the children of Adam, there is still more sacred union among the children of God."

[66] The First Geneva Convention For the Amelioration of the Condition of the Wounded and Sick, Article 12; The Second Geneva Conventions for the Amelioration of the Condition of Wounded, Sick and Shipwrecked Members of Armed Forces at Sea, Article 12.

[67] The First Geneva Convention For the Amelioration of the Condition of the Wounded and Sick, Article 12.

[68] Lev. 19:18; Matt. 22:39–40; and Mark 12:31.

enemies.[69] Likewise, considering the ethnic animosities that the Jewish people and the Samaritans held for each other during Christ's lifetime, such treatment of a wounded person without regard for their race, nationality or religion appears to reflect the neighbor-love that Christ was trying to teach the lawyer.[70]

Prisoners of War

Soldiers should be discriminating in their treatment of POWs because the Bible calls them to. In the same verse from Matthew 25 concerning the sick in the previous section, Jesus taught his followers to have compassion for Christian prisoners. Such good works, while directed towards Christian prisoners in the context of the final judgment, represent the generalized "good" that the Apostle Paul taught Christians to do not only for other Christians but for "everyone."[71]

Compassion towards prisoners does not mean that soldiers should release the prisoner since the prisoner would return to the battlefield to fight. For that reason, justice requires that force be used to detain and maintain the prisoner in detention until the conclusion of hostilities; however, compassion requires that soldiers should use no more force or harm than is necessary to detain.

If a privileged belligerent (i.e., a member of the armed forces or militia belonging to a state or a member of the *levee en masse*[72]) surrenders or is captured on the battlefield, then his status becomes that of a prisoner of war.[73] The Third Geneva Convention, the

69 Matt. 5:44.

70 Luke 10:29–37.

71 Gal. 6:10.

72 The Third Geneva Convention Relative to the Treatment of Prisoners of War, Article 4.

73 Article 4 of the Third Geneva Convention uses "prisoners of war" as a term of art that specifically includes persons who were "Members of the armed forces of a Party to the conflict" as well as members of organized militias that fulfill the conditions of formality recognized by regular armed forces such as the following:

Prisoner of War Convention, includes a multitude of protections, but the most important protections are those of humane treatment;[74] protection from violence intimidation, and insults;[75] and specific protections during interrogations.[76] Regarding interrogations, Article 17 states:

> No physical or mental torture, nor any other form of coercion, may be inflicted on prisoners of war to secure from them information of any kind whatever. Prisoners of war who refuse to answer may not be threatened, insulted, or exposed to any unpleasant or disadvantageous treatment of any kind.[77]

There is no exception to this rule for military necessity. For example, a soldier may capture an enemy soldier who knows the location of the sniper who is shooting his fellow combatants. The prohibition against physical and mental torture, coercion, and insults has no exception for military necessity. It is a deontological rule that does not allow for a utilitarian balancing of the lives of all his fellow soldiers against the discomfort of the single POW.

William V. O'Brien made several observations about the rationale behind the POW protections. Professor O'Brien wrote about

---

a) that of being commanded by a person responsible for his subordinates;

b) that of having a fixed distinctive sign recognizable at a distance;

c) that of carrying arms openly;

d) that of conducting their operations in accordance with the laws and customs of war.

This definition would not apply to Al Qaeda and Taliban detainees since they were not members of an armed force that was a party to the conflict or members of an organized militia with the four conditions. Accordingly, they were prisoners but not prisoners of war entitled to the protections of the Third Geneva Conventions.

[74] The Third Geneva Convention Relative to the Treatment of Prisoners of War, Article 13.

[75] Ibid.

[76] Ibid., Article 17.

[77] Ibid.

the reciprocity underlying the Convention in that "belligerents . . . treat enemy prisoners of war as they would like their own to be treated" because they are "intensely solicitous of the welfare of each and every one of [their] own" who could become a prisoner of war in the enemy's hands.[78] He also observed that the defenselessness of the POW is a motivating concern. The POW should be protected because he is no longer fighting and no longer a threat to anyone regardless of whatever intelligence value the prisoner might be withholding regarding the enemy's plans.[79] The same rationale supports the requirements for the humane treatment of unprivileged belligerents in Common Article 3.

Detainees Other Than POWs

Biblically, there is no difference between a POW and all other detainees or prisoners who fail to qualify for POW status because they were fighting outside of the categories in Article 4 of the Third Geneva Convention. The difference is a legal distinction without a theological difference. Nonetheless, the Geneva Conventions do make a legal distinction between POWs and all other detainees. The Third Geneva Convention provides many benefits to POWs to include advance pay in Swiss francs;[80] canteens where they may purchase tobacco;[81] opportunities for intellectual, educational, and recreational pursuits;[82] as well as opportunities to work and be paid.[83] Detainees who fail to meet the POW criteria do not receive those and other benefits, but they do receive the same, basic protection of humane treatment in the catch-all provision in Common Article 3 of the Geneva Conventions. Common Article 3 simply protects detainees

[78] O'Brien, *The Just Conduct of War*, 151.

[79] Ibid., 153.

[80] The Third Geneva Convention Relative to the Treatment of Prisoners of War, Article 60.

[81] Ibid., Article 28.

[82] Ibid., Article 38.

[83] Ibid., Section III.

from "violence to life and person . . . cruel treatment and torture" and "outrages upon personal dignity, in particular humiliating and degrading treatment."[84]

The Common Article 3 protections should have prohibited much of the treatment that was discussed in chapter 1: the waterboarding that caused detainees to physiologically react like a man drowning, the painful stress positions, the slaps, the rectal penetrations used as interrogation techniques, and the use of extreme temperatures. And the prohibition against cruel treatment, outrages upon personal dignity, and humiliating and degrading treatment should have prohibited the use of nakedness, sexual exploitation, and the treatment of detainees like animals. None of these techniques constitute humane treatment.

Christian theology provides the rationale why detainees should be protected from torture, violence, cruel treatment, outrages upon personal dignity, and humiliating treatment while detained. In Matthew 25, as discussed in the previous two sections, Jesus calls on his followers to do acts of charity for Christian prisoners, and in Galatians 6:10, Paul calls on Christians to do good works towards everyone inside and outside the household of faith.[85] Such good works should include the prisoner-mercy that Christ shows in his concern for Christian prisoners in Matthew 25.

Christians should have identified with the detainees in Iraq and Afghanistan and demonstrated enough compassion to treat them humanely. All persons are born with the same sinful condition[86] that can only be changed by the sacrificial compassion and mercy of Christ.[87] Fleming Rutledge has preached that Christians should identify with the detainees in Iraq and Afghanistan in the same way that John Bradford did when he saw a group of prisoners being led to

[84] Common Article 3 of the Geneva Conventions of 1949.
[85] Gal. 6:10.
[86] Rom. 3:23.
[87] Rom. 6:1–14.

the gallows.[88] Bradford said, "There but for the grace of God goes John Bradford," which is attributed to the more popular saying, "There but for the Grace of God go I."[89] This does not mean all sins are equal—they are not. This means that the American soldiers and national security officials should view the detainee with God's heart that includes justice and love. As the Apostle Paul wrote, "Christ Jesus came into the world to save sinners, of whom I am the foremost."[90] Christians should look at detainees, identify with them as fellow sinners, restrain them as justice requires, and treat them with mercy because the Christian received mercy.

Christians should also identify with the detainees in Iraq and Afghanistan because the Old Testament's Book of the Covenant revealed God's desire for his covenant people to identify with the weakest people in society such as the alien, the widow and the orphan.[91] These categories of people held the least power in society and were the most vulnerable to oppression. God cares for them so much that if someone takes advantage of them, and they cry out to Him, God's wrath will burn and He will avenge them.[92] The detainee from Iraq and Afghanistan should be considered to be even more vulnerable than anyone in the world. Once captured and restrained, either by restraints on their hands and feet or in a detention facility, the detainee is a defenseless person who cannot resist being attacked. Their captors have absolute control over every aspect of their lives: food, clothing, shelter, when they wake, when they sleep, whether they may relieve themselves in a toilet or in their clothing, and whether they may have access to the Bible or Koran. The captor's

[88] Fleming Rutledge, "My Enemy, Myself: A Sermon." in *Torture is a Moral Issue*, ed.George Hunsinger. (Grand Rapids: William B. Eerdmans, 2008), 114.

[89] Ibid..

[90] Rom. 5:6–8.

[91] Ex. 22:21–23.

[92] Ex. 22:24.

absolute control must be fettered by appropriate laws and regulations that will require humane treatment.

The Need for the Law among Fallen People

The columnist Charles Krauthammer once argued that al-Qaeda and Taliban detainees should not receive the protections against torture in the Geneva Conventions. He argued that they had forfeited the protections of the law of war since they were not members of a legitimate armed force that followed the laws of war but terrorists who had no regard for the laws of war.[93] Krauthammer's argument mistakenly assumed that the law's protections are handed out as a reward based upon the good conduct of soldiers. On the contrary, Krauthammer over-generalizes on the virtue of soldiers throughout history. All privileged belligerents receive POW status regardless of whether they fight justly or criminally. Just war philosopher Darrell Cole responded to Krauthammer's argument by pointing out that

> When we start comparing the captured terrorist with, say, a captured SS officer, the term "legitimacy" begins to lose its moral force. The evil represented by the SS officer is not one wit smaller than the evil represented by the Islamic fundamentalist. In fact, unlike the Islamic fundamentalist, the evil represented by the SS officer had a real chance to conquer what Churchill could still refer to as "The Christian West." Why do we privilege the Nazi simply because he has the good fortune to be an enlisted officer in a recognized nation state?"[94]

[93] Charles Krauthammer, "The Truth About Torture: It's time to be honest about doing terrible things," *Weekly Standard* (Dec. 5, 2005), http://www.weeklystandard.com/the-truth-about-torture/article/7589.

[94] Darrell Cole, "Darrell Cole on Torture," *First Things* (Jan. 6, 2010), http://www.firstthings.com/blogs/first thoughts/2010/01/darrell-cole-on-torture.

Cole's point is that we do not decide whether to protect POWs and detainees based upon their good conduct or bad conduct. We protect both POWs and detainees because of the captor's potential for bad conduct. Detainees must be protected from their sinful, fallen captors who will not receive perfect natures until they are born again and reach the new heavens and the new Earth at the end of time.

Gary Haugen, the CEO of International Justice Mission, understood that the need for protections in law arises from the overwhelming power of the state and captors.

> Because the power of the state over detainees is exercised by fallen human beings, that power must be limited by clear boundaries, and individuals exercising such power must be transparently accountable. Therefore, even if it is expedient to inflict cruelty and degradation on a prisoner during interrogation . . . the moral teachings of Christ, the Torah and the Prophets do not permit it.[95]

Haugen appears to make the point that John Calvin established regarding the second use of the law.[96] Calvin wrote that the second use of the law is to curb sin among fallen people whose minds might not be inwardly conformed to the values underpinning the law but whose hands should obey it out of compulsion.[97] Citing the Apostle Paul's instructions to Timothy about this use of the law in 1 Timothy 1:8–10, Calvin believes that the law serves as a restraint on the unruly lusts that would burst forth otherwise.[98]

This appears to be what occurred in the mistreatment of detainees when President Bush removed the protections of the Geneva

[95] Gary Haugen, "Silence on Suffering," *Christianity Today* (October 17, 2005), http://www.christianitytoday. com/ct/2005/octoberweb-only/12.0b.html.

[96] Calvin, *Institutes*, 2.7.10–11.

[97] Ibid., 2.7.10.

[98] Ibid.; 1 Tim. 1:8–10.

Conventions and even the minimal protections of Common Article 3. In the drive to obtain intelligence and national security after the attacks of September 11th, President Bush removed the law of war protections, which many people understood to be license to change the treatment of detainees. As discussed in chapter 1, the head of the CIA Counterterrorism Center believed that the gloves had come off and that the rules on detainee treatment had changed. But many people failed to appreciate that nothing had changed in the sinful condition of the human heart that the law had restrained.

Conclusion

One of the purposes of the just war tradition is to take Christian love and to make it incarnational[99] by developing practical, moral guidelines useful in the military service of soldiers on the battlefield.[100] The just war tradition takes Christian teachings and applies them to aggression and oppression on the battlefield in order to find practical principles that guide warriors.[101]

The principle of discrimination provides the "twin-born" justification for war and limitation on war.[102] A Christian soldier's loving regard for his neighbors and the state's demands of justice compel him to fight wars of self-defense against aggressors who would oppress his neighbors. But once his enemies have been captured and are *hors de combat*, the Christian soldier must respect and protect detainees out of Christ's requirement that Christians love their enemies[103] and show mercy towards prisoners.[104] In order to ensure righteous conduct by captors, states must also have protections in law that will protect the detainee from his captors who carry the same fallen condition that he

[99] Ramsey, *The Just War*, 164.
[100] O'Brien, *The Just Conduct of War*, 5.
[101] Ramsey, *The Just War*, 151.
[102] Ibid., 164.
[103] Matt. 5:43–46; Rom. 5:10; Rom. 12:17–24.
[104] Matt. 25:34–40; Gal. 6:10.

carries. But understanding that the law may fail, theologians, pastors (local theologians), and military ethicists standing in the just war tradition must prepare Christians and soldiers with a theology or professional military education that is robust enough to stop misconduct when the law fails.

4

The Proportionality of Methods That Attack the *Imago Dei*

We were created in his image, and we owe each other a certain level of dignity—a certain level of respect. And that's just a line we can't cross. . . . Scripture talks a lot about human dignity and the sanctity of human life. And it's there for a reason. That's a big issue for God, it seems. And if it's a big issue for him, then we better have it as a big issue for us.[1]

Proportionality is the second of the two *jus in bello* principles.[2] It asks whether a proposed method of warfare is proportional to the military or political end being pursued.[3] In the seventeenth century, Hugo Grotius argued that justice required that the punishment be proportionate to the evil that the aggressor has caused.[4] Put in the

[1] Marine Lieutenant Colonel Stuart Couch, the military commissions prosecutor for Mohamedou Ould Slahi. Stuart Couch, Interview, *Torturing Democracy*, National Security Archive/Washington Media Associates, October 9, 2007, http://nsarchive.gwu.edu/torturingdemocracy/interviews/stuart_couch.html.

[2] James Turner Johnson, *Ideology, Reason, and the Limitation of War* (Princeton, NJ: Princeton University Press, 1999), 18; William V. O'Brien. *The Conduct of Just and Limited War* (New York: Praeger Publishers, 1981), 37.

[3] O'Brien, *The Conduct of Just and Limited War*, 37.

[4] Hugo Grotius, *Law of War and Peace*, vol. 2, trans. A.C. Campbell, (Kitchener, ON: Batoche Books, 2001), 182, 187, 200,

specific context of democratic statecraft, or the use of military force by democratic states to preserve not only the state but the values that the state represents, Paul Ramsey defined proportionality as force that is "no more than the force needed effectively to protect the endangered values" that are threatened by the aggressor while reconciling "those values against the values that will be destroyed in the course of that same use of force."[5] Ramsey argues that justice requires states to harmonize the national common good to the common good of all men and nations because "the traditional principle of proportionality always assumed that there might be some costs too great."[6] In other words, preservation of the state cannot be considered "a supreme value for men" that justifies no limits on their methods of warfare.[7]

As such, the international community and Christian theologians have deemed some methods of warfare to be so morally disproportionate to any conceivable end that could be sought that the methods are deemed to be *mala in se* (i.e., methods morally wrong in themselves).[8] Such methods of warfare are so "morally repugnant that it would never be proportional to any end sought."[9] The Catechism of the Catholic Church provides an example in "the extermination of a people, nation, or ethnic minority" or genocide as one method of warfare commonly accepted as *mala in se*.

Interrogational torture is another method of warfare that has been determined to be *mala in se* by both law and just war philosophers.[10] There are abundant examples in law, but the premier example is in Article 2 of the U.N. Convention Against Torture, ratified by

---

http://socserv2.socsci.mcmaster.ca/econ/ugcm/3ll3/grotius/Law2.pdf.

[5] Ramsey, *The Just War*, 403.

[6] Ibid., 405.

[7] Ibid.

[8] Brian Orend, *The Morality of Warfare* (Toronto: Broadview Press, 2006), 123.

[9] James Turner Johnson, *Morality and Contemporary Warfare* (New Haven: Yale University Press, 1999), 29.

[10] James Turner Johnson, "Torture: A Just War Perspective," *The Review of Faith & International Affairs* 5, 2 (2007): 31.

the U.S. Senate in 1994, which states, "No exceptional circumstances whatsoever, whether a state of war or a threat of war, internal political instability or any other public emergency, may be invoked as a justification of torture."[11] James Turner Johnson, the preeminent contemporary just war philosopher, has determined that torture is "so morally repugnant" to the just war tradition that it "should never be morally allowed."[12]

This chapter will reason that the torture and mistreatment of detainees during interrogations is *mala in se* because it violates the *Imago Dei* (i.e., the image of God) in two persons: (1) the *Imago Dei* in the detainee and (2) the Image of Christ in the Christian interrogator or national security official approving of interrogation having an effect that falls into any of the 5 groups documented in chapter 1: (1) pain and physical abuse, (2) sexual exploitation, (3) religious exploitation, (4) extreme sensory deprivation, sleep deprivation, and isolation to the point it assaulted a detainees ability to reason, and (5) the treatment of detainees like animals.

First, this chapter will address the *Imago Dei* in detainees and discuss how the treatment of some detainees violated the image of God in them. Secondly, this book will address the *Imago Dei* in Christian interrogators and how the treatment of some detainees could have violated the image of Christ in the Christian interrogator.

Basis for the *Imago Dei* in Detainees

The biblical basis for seeing the *Imago Dei* in a person begins with Genesis 1:26–27, where God says:

> "Let us make man in our image, after our likeness. And let them have dominion over the fish of the sea and over the fly-

[11] Convention against Torture and Other Cruel, Inhuman or Degrading Treatment or Punishment Article 2 (December 12, 1984).

[12] Johnson, *Morality and Contemporary Warfare*, 29.

> ing creatures of the sky and over the beasts and over the whole earth and over all the creeping things that creeps on the earth." Then God created man in his own image, in the image of God he created him; male and female he created them.[13]

In this passage, God breaks from the pattern of creating by command and chooses to deliberate in consultation regarding His last creation.[14] Unlike all the other animals, God chooses to make men and women in his own image and likeness and to make them his vice-regents over the rest of His creation.[15] This notion that men and women have the honor and dignity of being God's image bearer and representative on the earth is reinforced by Psalm 8, which Anthony Hoekema finds to be a "lyric echo" of Genesis 1:26–27.[16]

> Yet you have made him a little lower than the heavenly beings and crowned him with glory and honor. You have given him dominion over the works of your hands. You have put all things under his feet, all sheep and oxen, and also the beasts of the field, the birds of the heavens, and the fish of the sea, whatever passes along the paths of the seas.[17]

Of these verses, Calvin sees the psalmist, David, celebrating the special favor that God showed mankind during creation, by making them his representatives and a mirror in which we can behold God's own glory.[18]

[13] Gen. 1:26–27 (the author's translation).

[14] John Calvin, *Commentaries on the First Book of Moses Called Genesis*, vol. 1 (Grand Rapids: Baker Books, 2005), 91.

[15] Ibid., 94.

[16] Anthony A. Hoekema, *Created in God's Image* (Grand Rapids: Wm. B. Eerdmans, 1986), 19 (attributing this to Franz Delitzsch as quoted by other authors).

[17] Ps. 8:5–8.

[18] Calvin, *Commentary Upon The Book of Psalms* (Grand Rapids: Baker Books, 2005), 93–94.

The fact that each person carries the *Imago Dei* has implications for how people should treat each other. This is made plain when God speaks to Noah and his sons after they have disembarked and are poised to reestablish civilization. God states, "The man shedding the blood of man, his blood will be poured out by man, for in his image God made man."[19] Here God uses murder, the greatest mistreatment of one person by another, to explain that his great concern for men and women stems from the fact that they bear His image. Anthony Hoekema understands this verse to say, "To touch the image of God is to touch God himself,"[20] therefore God puts himself in the shoes of victims and takes great personal offense at mistreatment.

Finally, Christ made express the implications of the Old Testament's prohibitions against murder when He showed that they were emblematic for all mistreatment—even insults.

> You have heard that it was said to those of old, 'You shall not murder; and whoever murders will be liable to judgment.' But I say to you that everyone who is angry with his brother will be liable to judgment; whoever insults his brother will be liable to the council; and whoever says, 'You fool!' will be liable to the hell of fire.[21]

Accordingly, the Heidelberg Catechism finds the teaching of these Scriptures and many others to be that people should not "belittle, hate, insult, or kill" their neighbors by their thoughts, words or deeds;[22] and the Westminster Larger Catechism additionally sees prohibitions against "oppression, quarreling, striking, wounding"[23] among other acts of mistreatment.

[19] Gen. 9:6.
[20] Hoekema, *Created in God's Image*, 16.
[21] Matt. 5:21–22.
[22] HC 105.
[23] WLC 136.

All Persons Carry the *Imago Dei*

The Bible teaches that all persons carry the *Imago Dei.* The fact that God created Adam and Eve in his image before their fall into sin has caused theologians to wrestle with whether the image survived the fall and whether all people can be considered to carry the *Imago Dei.* Calvin believed that mankind's fall into sin brought great "corruption and degradation" to the image of God in humans,[24] corrupting man's uncorrupted nature,[25] and leaving him with a depraved nature.[26] However, Calvin found that theologians must "grant that the image of God was not utterly defaced and destroyed in him"[27] and "is not altogether extinguished."[28] Calvin believed that "we can trace some remains of divine image distinguishing the whole human race."[29]

Calvin's beliefs reflect passages from both the Old and New Testament where God speaks of men born after the fall as carrying the *Imago Dei.* Such passages include the following:

- Genesis 5:1–3, in which God links His image in Adam as continuing in Adam's son Seth who was born "in his likeness, like his image;"[30]
- Genesis 9:5–6, in which God tells Noah and his sons that murder shall be punished because man continues to be made in God's own image;
- Psalm 8:5, in which David appears to celebrate God's extension of "His excellence and heavenly dignity" to all of mankind;[31] and

[24] Calvin, *Institutes* 1.15.1.
[25] Calvin, *Commentary Upon The Book of Psalms*, 104n1.
[26] Calvin, *Institutes*, 1.15.1.
[27] Ibid., 1.15.4.
[28] Calvin, *Commentary Upon The Book of Psalms*, 104.
[29] Calvin, *Institutes*, 2.2.17.
[30] Gen. 5:3.
[31] Calvin, *Commentary Upon the Book of Psalms*, 104.

- James 3:9, in which Christians are taught to not to curse other people because they were "made in the likeness of God."[32]

With regard to James's use of the Greek word for "made," Hoekema finds that God's past action of making men and women in His image continues to have an effect on the way we treat all people today.[33]

Do Terrorists, Detainees, and Other Criminals Carry the *Imago Dei*?

The question may remain: Do terrorists, detainees suspected of terrorism, or even convicted criminals who have committed great atrocities, carry the image of God? As discussed in the previous section, Genesis 5:1–3 teaches that all of the generations that have been born of Adam since the fall carry the *Imago Dei*. Christ[34] and James[35] both taught that Christians should treat all persons as if they are the *Imago Dei* without making any exception for great criminals. G. C. Berkower found that the greatest sinners in the Bible wrote about their sinfulness with deep seriousness but without any indication that it destroyed their essential humanity.[36] Berkouwer pointed to the Apostle Paul, who described himself as continuing to be "the foremost" of all sinners[37] yet continued to bear the Image of Christ. He also pointed to the Psalmist Asaph, who judged his sinful actions as brutish and ignorant and like those of a "beast,"[38] but Asaph clearly meant that only metaphorically since he indicated that he continued to bear the Image of God. Berkouwer understood these descriptions

[32] James 3:9.
[33] Hoekema, *Created in God's Image*, 20.
[34] Matt. 5:21–22.
[35] James 3:9.
[36] G. C. Berkouwer, *Man: The Image of God* (Grand Rapids: Wm. B. Eerdmans, 1962), 190.
[37] 1 Tim. 1:15.
[38] Ps. 73:21–23.

not as descriptions of non-humanness but "a humanness up to its sinful limits."[39]

In addition to the greatest sinners, Berkouwer argued that the Bible even described some men as operating under the direct influence of Satan while still retaining their humanity. Berkouwer pointed to the Apostle Peter, to whom Christ said in Matthew 16:23, "Get behind me, Satan!"; Judas, of whom Luke described as having Satan inside of him in Luke 22:3; and the antichrist, who Paul described in 2 Thessalonians 2:3 as the "man of lawlessness."[40] From all of these passages, the clear implication is that the greatest sinners—even those operating as agents of Satan—have not lost their humanity. If the greatest sinners in biblical history retained their humanity, then this book argues that convicted terrorists and, even more so, detainees suspected of terrorism retain theirs. All of them carry the *Imago Dei* and must be treated accordingly.

What Is the *Imago Dei* in the Detainee and How Was It Violated?

Understanding that detainees suspected of terrorism retain the *Imago Dei*, this section will discuss the practical characteristics of the *Imago Dei* and provide examples of detainee mistreatment that have violated the *Imago Dei*. Christian theologians have "long puzzled" over the issue and have written many books trying to specifically determine the characteristics of a person that are the *Imago Dei*.[41] The answers are like varying perspectives of the same object. The remainder of this chapter will use John Calvin's perspective of the *Imago Dei* since it sets forth the "Reformation understanding"[42] of the *Imago Dei*

[39] Berkouwer, *Man: The Image of God*, 190.

[40] Ibid., 191.

[41] John M. Frame, *Systematic Theology* (Phillipsburg, NJ: P&R Publishing, 2013), 784.

[42] Stanley J. Grenz, *The Social God and the Relational Self* (Louisville: Westminster John Knox Press, 2001), 166.

that most subsequent theologians have started with when further developing their understanding.

Calvin begins by arguing that man is both a body and a spirit.[43] Calvin favors the spirit as the proper seat for the *Imago Dei* because those aspects are more easily discernible, but Calvin believed that man's physical body also reflected the *Imago Dei* since Christ's human body was the *Imago Dei*.[44] Calvin taught that "there is no part of the body in which some rays of glory did not shine"[45] forth from creation like vestiges from before man's fall into sin.[46] Regarding the spirit, Calvin argued that the *Imago Dei* extends to each characteristic "in which the nature of man surpasses that of all other species of animals."[47] Those characteristics include a person's reason, ability to form moral judgments over good and evil, the seeds of religion that enable us to relate to God, the ability to relate to other persons especially in marriage, and the conscience that give us the ability to sense shame.[48] With regard to warfare and detainee mistreatment, this section will first consider the implications of the *Imago Dei* in the body and then the spirit.

[43] Calvin, *Institutes*, 1.15.2. Calvin believes that soul and spirit mean different things but are often used together as "equivalents." He cites examples of Christ and Stephen who commended their spirits to God when they were dying as well as the spirit's return to God upon death in Ecclesiastes 12:7. John Frame finds that Scripture does not distinguish spirit, soul, and body as different metaphysical components of man; rather, they are different perspectives of considering a person. John M. Frame, *Systematic Theology*, 784.

[44] Calvin, *Institutes*, 1.15.3.

[45] Ibid.

[46] Berkouwer, *Man: The Image of God*, 76.

[47] Calvin, *Institutes*, 1.15.3 and 2.2.17.

[48] Calvin, *Commentary Upon the Psalms*, 102; Wayne Grudem, *Systematic Theology* (Grand Rapids: Zondervan, 2000), 446–48.

The Imago Dei *in the Human Body*

The image of God extends to the human body as evidenced in Genesis 9:6, which provides that murder is the destruction of the image of God.[49] Herman Bavinck found that the human body is God's "wondrous masterpiece" that is as essential to the image of God as the soul.[50] Bavinck reasoned that "God could not have been able to become a man if he had not first made man in his own image."[51] The implications of the *Imago Dei* being in the human body must be considered with regard to warfare in the following respects: (a) killing during war and (b) the state's purposeful infliction of pain during interrogation for the purpose of getting intelligence.

Just Warriors Are the Imago Dei

God is a warrior and people bear His image when they engage in just wars. As discussed in chapter 3, the state has God's authority to keep order and punish wrongdoers, whether they are common criminals or enemies of an aggressor state.[52] This authority is founded upon God's giving the state the power of the sword to punish the wrongdoer whether he is a house robber or a foreign army that has come to plunder and oppress the entire state.[53] The state cannot exercise the power of the sword unless soldiers wield it. The Book of Exodus presents God himself as a "man of war" who killed Pharaoh's chosen officers and his host of chariots when He cast them into the sea and they were sunk.[54] David, a man after God's own heart, is

[49] Louis Berkoff, *Systematic Theology* (Grand Rapids: William B. Eerdmans, 1996), 205.

[50] Hoekema, *Created in God's Image*, 68 (quoting Herman Bavinck from Hoekema's own translation of *Reformed Dogmatics*, 2:602).

[51] Herman Bavinck, *Reformed Dogmatics*, ed. John Bolt, trans. John Vriend, vol. 2, (Grand Rapids: Baker Academic, 2004) 560–61.

[52] Calvin, *Institutes*, 4.20.11; Rom. 13:3–4.

[53] Calvin, *Institutes*, 4.20.11; Rom. 13:3–4; 1 Peter 2:13–17.

[54] Ex. 15:3; See also Isa. 42:13 where God is described as "like a mighty man, like a man of war."

presented as faithful in killing tens of thousands of Philistines.[55] And in Revelation 19, the Apostle John describes seeing God's son, the ascended and glorified Jesus Christ, appearing as a man of war, mounted on a horse, wearing a robe dipped in blood, in command of the armies of heaven, fighting the final battle against the enemies of God who have been oppressing His church, and slaying enemies with the sword that came from his mouth.[56] In all of these inspired Scriptures, written by different human authors, the Holy Spirit is communicating that God is a warrior and that man is in His image when he engages in just wars. As discussed in chapter 2, those wars are ones in which the soldier fights (1) in self defense of his neighbors out of his love for them and (2) for the state in a demand for justice against the wrongdoers who would oppress and plunder their state.

Pain and Physical Abuse of Detainees as an Assault on the Imago Dei

Yet the same love that provided the justification to use force against aggressors also provides a limitation on the use of force once the enemy's aggression has ceased.[57] This is the "paradox of love and wrath...found in the character of God himself."[58] So the wartime killing of soldiers by other soldiers does not violate Genesis 9:6 and the *Imago Dei* considering the biblical precedents (i.e., God, Abraham, the Judges of Israel, David, and Jesus discussed above), but there is no biblical warrant for physical abuse and the purposeful imposition of pain on prisoners during wartime.[59] Even outside of wartime, the

[55] 1 Sam. 18:7.

[56] Rev. 19:11–21.

[57] Ramsey, *The Just War*, 144.

[58] Davis, *Evangelical Ethics*, 251.

[59] Tyler Wigg-Stevenson, "Tortured Truth," in *Religious Faith, Torture, and Our National Soul*, ed. David P. Gushee (Macon, GA: Mercer University Press, 2010), 144–45. "Some practices, like torture, exceed the authority granted to government by God. To endorse torture is to perpetuate the untruth that the nation is more than god has made it to be. . . . Human government is simply not important enough to justify the violation of God's

only Scriptural precedent for permitting the state to impose pain on the human body is the sentence of forty lashes permitted after the due process of a criminal trial in which the criminal is found guilty and sentenced by a judge.[60] Yet the forty lashes can be distinguished in two respects from the methods of pain infliction that that were designed by national security officials and imposed by interrogators between 2002 and 2006.

First, the use of pain to extract intelligence was imposed not upon convicted criminals but upon mere suspects. The sword of Romans 13:3–4 should not be understood as a symbol of interrogational pain or physical abuse. This is best demonstrated in Acts 22:22–30 when the Roman tribune rescinds his order (i.e., that Paul "should be examined by flogging, to find out" what crime he had committed) when he finds out that Paul (the author of Romans 13:3–4) is a Roman citizen.[61] The readers of Paul's epistle to the Romans would have only understood the sword in Romans 13:3–4 to represent the ruler's "penal prerogative"[62] to punish those who have been judged to be guilty, which is a different context from the whip of interrogational torture. James D. G. Dunn concurs that the sword could not have been a symbol of pre-trial corporal punishment to Paul's Roman readers since they "had the right of appeal to a higher court and as far as the emperor."[63] Accordingly, the wrongdoer could only be a person who has been found guilty of wrongdoing in order to deserve the punishment of the ruler's sword. Dietrich Bonhoeffer emphasizes this distinction as the key difference between "retributive punishment" of a guilty person and the "infliction of pain while taking advantage of a relative superiority of strength, and in particular the extortion by this

---

law." Ibid.

[60] Deut. 25:1–3.

[61] Acts 22:25.

[62] John Murray, *Principles of Conduct: Aspects of Biblical Ethics* (Grand Rapids: Wm. B. Eerdmans, 1957), 153.

[63] James D. G. Dunn, *Romans 9–16*, vol. 38b (Dallas: Word Books, 1988), 764 citing Acts 25:11.

means of some desired admission or statement."[64] Bonhoeffer finds that the latter use of pain is a misuse of the human body for the achievement of another man's purpose in the detainee's body.[65]

The second distinction between the use of pain as a punishment and the use of pain as a method of interrogation is that the 40 lashes were a set limit while the examples of interrogational torture in chapter 1 continued for days and, in some cases, months. Secretary Rumsfeld approved a request to use stress positions for up to four hours, but offered to permit more upon request—evidence that the only limit was Secretary Rumsfeld's unfettered discretion.[66] Khalid Sheik Mohammed was reportedly waterboarded 183 times with no apparent limit imposed until he relented and provided intelligence.[67]

Some scholars have reasoned that the use pain for interrogational purposes (e.g., waterboarding to induce a physical sensation of drowning and the use of stress positions) violates the *Imago Dei* in a person's physical body because the interrogator's will invades the integrity of the detainee's body in the form of pain in order to turn the body against the spirit's will to withhold intelligence.[68] The pain

[64] Dietrich Bonhoeffer, *Ethics*, trans. Neville Horton Smith (New York: Simon & Schuster, 1995), 183.

[65] Ibid.

[66] Donald Rumsfeld, "Counter Resistance Techniques" (Dec. 2, 2002), http://nsarchive.gwu.edu/torturing democracy/documents/20021127-1.pdf ; James T. Hill, "Counter-Resistance Techniques" (Oct. 25, 2002), http://nsarchive. gwu.edu/torturingdemocracy/documents/20021025.pdf; Major General Michael Dunlavey, "Counter-Resistance Strategies" (Oct. 11, 2002), http://nsarchive.gwu.edu/torturingdemocracy/documents/ 20021011.pdf; Jay S. Bybee, Memo, "Interrogation of al Qaeda Operative" (Aug 1, 2002): 3–4, http://nsarchive.gwu.edu/torturingdemocracy/ documents/20020122.pdf .

[67] Scott Shane, "Waterboarding used 266 times on 2 Suspects" *New York Times*, April 19, 2009, http://www. nytimes.com/2009/04/20/world/20detain.html?_r=0.

[68] Derek S. Jeffreys, *Spirituality and the Ethics of Torture* (New York: Palgrave Macmillan, 2009), 72.

invades the person as a foreign presence expressing someone else's will from the inside.[69] Dietrich Bonhoeffer wrote,

> The Human Body must never become a thing, an object, such as might fall under the unrestricted power of another man and be used by him solely as a means to his own ends. The living human body is always the man himself. Rape, exploitation, torture, and arbitrary confinement of the human body are serious violations of the right which is given with the creation of man.[70]

Torture assaults and perverts the autonomy with which the person was created by God.[71]

There is a temptation to find irony in that killing during a just war does not assault the *Imago Dei* while torture—which results in temporary pain short of permanent death—would be an assault on the *Imago Dei*. A distinct aspect of Augustine's approach to just war was his lack of concern for death compared to his great concern for cruelty and domination of the living.[72]

> What is it about war that is to be blamed? Is it that those who will die someday are killed . . . ? That is the complaint of the timid not the Christian. The desire for harming, the cruelty of revenge, the restless and implacable mind, the savageness of revolting, the lust for dominating, and similar things—these are what are justly blamed in wars.[73]

[69] Ibid., 62.

[70] Bonhoeffer, *Ethics*, 181.

[71] Jeffreys, *Spirituality and the Ethics of Torture*, 62.

[72] David D. Corey and J. Daryl Charles, *The Just War Tradition* (Wilmington, DE: Intercollegiate Studies Institute, 2012), 63.

[73] Augustine, "Against Faustus the Manichean XXII.73–79" in *Augustine: Political Writings*, trans. Michael W. Tkacz and Douglas Kries (Indianapolis, IN: Hacket Publishing, 1994), 221.

Death is a condition all persons will experience, but cruelty is not. Augustine appears to believe that the Christian soldier need not be timid in combat because death allows the person's spirit to escape the body and return to God.[74] On the other hand, the cruelty, savagery, and domination of torture trap the soul in a bodily prison of pain with no ability to escape or resist. The person undergoing interrogational pain has no defenses and no escape from the interrogator on the outside and the pain on the inside. The detainee's spirit is under total oppression.

Assaults on the Imago Dei *in a Detainee's Spirit*

As previously discussed, a person's spirit is the *Imago Dei* in those characteristics that distinguish the person with greater capabilities from the rest of the animals and creation. Those characteristics include a person's reason, ability to form moral judgments over good and evil, the seeds of religion that enable us to approach God and relate to him, the ability to relate to other persons especially in marriage, and the conscience that give us the ability to sense shame.[75] The following sections will consider each of these characteristics in relation to the mistreatment of detainees and argue (a) that the use of nakedness and sexual exploitation were assaults on the *Imago Dei* in a detainee's sense of shame, (b) that the use of sleep deprivation was an assault upon the *Imago Dei* in a detainee's ability to reason, (c) that the use of sexually derogatory insults and threats to cause the rape of family exploited the *Imago Dei* in family relationships, and (d) that the use of dog collars and other techniques sought to remove the dignity of the *Imago Dei* from the detainee and reduce him to the level of the other animals.

[74] 2 Cor. 5:6, 8.

[75] Calvin, *Commentary Upon the Book of Psalms*, 102; Grudem, *Systematic Theology*, 446–48.

Nakedness and Sexual Exploitation as Assaults on the Imago Dei

The use of nakedness and other techniques of sexual exploitation were assaults on the *Imago Dei* in detainees and their sense of shame as well as their ability to approach their god. The human body is the *Imago Dei*, but for a person to have their nakedness involuntarily exhibited to others is an assault on the *Imago Dei* in the person's spirit. Forced nakedness dehumanizes the naked person in the eyes of those who view his body without any barrier. After the fall, Adam and Eve ran away and hid from God, seeking to make clothes out of fig leaves, because their nakedness made them feel shame and fear.[76] The feeling of shame and fear was not unique to Adam and Eve in front of God, but is the common human reaction to involuntary nakedness. Shem's shaming of his father Noah's nakedness led to Noah cursing Shem while blessing the other sons who faithfully honored their father by covering his nakedness without looking upon him.[77]

Nakedness

Clothing allows people to cover their nakedness and make it part of their interior life[78] that should only be revealed in the most intimate, trusting moments of the marriage relationship or other voluntary occasions such as a locker room where all persons are peers and equally naked without anyone in a position of oppression. Being forced into nakedness by enemy captors who hold positions of authority, force, and control, is to remove the protection that clothing provides.[79] Nakedness rips open the realm of secrecy[80] for others to measure, assess, and judge with their eyes that hold no love and charity like a spouse. To remove a person's clothes is to remove the authority that God gives all persons over their bodies and the most

[76] Gen. 3:10.
[77] Gen. 9:20–27.
[78] Jeffreys, *Spirituality and the Ethics of Torture*, 69.
[79] Ibid.
[80] Ibid.

personal decision over to whom that person will reveal their nakedness.[81]

Secretary Rumsfeld approved the use of nakedness as an interrogation technique,[82] and there is ample evidence of interrogators using it to break a detainee's will to resist. Al-Qahtani's interrogator's recorded in a log that "the detainee was strip searched. Initially he was attempting to resist the guards. After approximately five minutes of nudity the detainee ceased to resist. . . . He stated that he did not like females viewing his naked body while being searched."[83] A Department of Defenses (DoD) Independent Panel determined that "the widespread practice of stripping detainees . . . evolved into something much broader, resulting in a practice of groups of detainees being kept naked [together] for extended periods of time at Abu Ghraib."[84] The DoD Independent Panel found that "the wearing of clothes is an inherently social practice" that when stripped away "had the unintended consequence of dehumanizing detainees in the eyes of those who interacted with them."[85]

Numerous investigations and reports document the consequences of dehumanization in a world without restraints upon state actors. The pictures out of Abu Ghraib showed naked detainees stacked into human pyramids like logs rather than humans. It showed naked detainees posed in sexually humiliating positions while soldiers posed in front of them. The International Committee for the Red Cross documented cases of detainees at Abu Ghraib being paraded in front of other detainees while naked with women's underwear on their

[81] Ibid., 70.

[82] Phifer, "Request for Approval of Counter-Resistance Strategies."

[83] Unknown Interrogator, "Interrogation Log Detainee 063" (23 November 2002),
http://nsarchive.gwu.edu/torturingdemocracy/documents/20031123.pdf.

[84] Independent Panel to Review DoD Detention Operations, *Final Report* (August 2004), 973, http://nsarchive.gwu.edu/torturingdemocracy/documents/20040824.pdf.

[85] Ibid.

heads and being forced to stand naked while female guards laughed at them and photographed them.[86] U.S. Army Major General Antonio Taguba conducted the first investigation into the treatment of detainees at Abu Ghraib in which he found evidence of "numerous incidents of sadistic, blatant, and wanton criminal abuses . . . [and] systemic and illegal abuse."[87] Those abuses included the following:

- Forcing male detainees to pose in the nude while female guards pointed at their genitals,
- Forcing female detainees to expose their breasts to the guards,
- Forcing detainees to perform indecent acts with each other,
- A video of a male American soldier in uniform sodomizing a female detainee,
- Handcuffing a naked detainee who was lying down on a wet floor, while an interrogator forced things into his rectum.[88]

Major General Taguba's Report included a detainee's narrative of the sexual exploitation of a father and son in which soldiers brought the two hooded detainees together. "They were both naked. They put them in front of each other and they counted 1, 2, 3, and then removed the bags from their heads. When the son saw his father naked, he was crying. He was crying because of seeing his father."[89]

[86] International Committee of the Red Cross, "Report of the International Committee of the Red Cross (ICRC) on the Treatment of Prisoners of War by Coalition Personnel and other Protected Persons by the Geneva Conventions in Iraq during Arrest, Internment, and Interrogation," in *The Torture Papers* ed. Karen Greenberg and Joshua Dratel, (Caimbridge: Caimbridge University Press 2006), 392.

[87] Major General Antonio M. Taguba, "Article 15–6 Investigation of the 800th Military Police Brigade," 16, http://nsarchive.gwu.edu/NSAEBB/NSAEBB140/TR3.pdf.

[88] Seymour Hersh, "The General's Report," *New Yorker* (June 25, 2007), http://www.newyorker.com/magazine/ 2007/06/25/the-generals-report.

[89] Jeffreys, *Spirituality and the Ethics of Torture*, 71 (citing the Taguba Report, p. 505); Scott Higham and Joe Stephens, "New Details of Prisoner Abuse Emerge" *Washington Post*, May 21, 2004),

Sexual Exploitation of Covenantal Relationships

To be created human is to be placed into a web of covenantal relationships that run not only vertically to God but horizontally toward other people such as parents, a spouse, children, and neighbors.[90] God created man as "male and female"[91] because it is not good for man be alone.[92] God created Adam and placed him in a covenantal relationship with Eve and commanded them to multiply into more covenantal relationships with children.[93] Just as God's nature is to be in a Trinitarian relationship, God created man's nature to live within a web of relationships.

For an interrogator to sexually exploit a detainee's covenantal relationships is to assault the *Imago Dei* in the detainee. Those whom Lieutenant Colonel Couch found to have threatened Slahi with the rape of his mother (by other detainees)[94] exploited Slahi's God given impulse to love and protect his mother. They deceived Slahi with threats of criminal conduct that exploited the covenantal relationships that God placed Slahi inside. Similarly, placing a naked father and son in front of each other so as to humiliate them is to tear at the *Imago Dei* in their relationship.[95] These actions mock God's created order of covenantal living and the *Imago Dei* of those he places in those relationships.

---

https://www.washingtonpost.com/archive/politics/2004/05/21/new-details-of-prison-abuse-emerge/7346e4cb-47f8-42ab-8897-38a021a1bd0c/; Prisoner Interview/Interrogation Team, "Translation of Statement Provided by Mohanded Juma JUMA, Detainee # 152307" http://media.washingtonpost.com/wp-srv/world/iraq/abughraib/152307.pdf.

[90] Michael Horton, *The Christian Fatih: A Systematic Theology* (Grand Rapids: Zondervan, 2011), 380.

[91] Gen. 1:27.

[92] Gen. 2:18.

[93] Gen. 1:27.

[94] Jess Bravin, *Terror Courts* (New Haven, CT: Yale University Press, 2013), 142.

[95] Sworn Statement by a Detainee in *The Torture Papers: The Road to Abu Ghraib*, ed. Karen Greenberg and Joshua L. Dratel (New York: Caimbridge University Press, 2005), 505.

The combination of nakedness and sexual exploitation leads into this chapter's next section on the *Imago Dei* in a person's relationship with God. Sexual exploitation uses the human body to induce feelings of shame, guilt and sin that interfere with the detainee's ability to approach his god.

Religious Exploitation to Deny a Detainee's Ability to Approach God

God created humans with hearts that were directed towards Him and an instinct to live *coram deo*—before the face of God.[96] Augustine expressed this when he wrote, "Thou hast made us for thyself, and our hearts are restless until they find their rest in you."[97] During times of trial, people reach out for strength and sovereign intervention from the God who made them and sees them.

Interrogators can block that source of strength by (1) attempting to stop a detainee from praying or (2) inducing feelings of shame and sin that cause the detainee to stop praying out of a sense of separation from their god.[98] As discussed in chapter 1, the U.S. Senate Armed Services Committee determined that the Defense Intelligence Agency intended to exploit Slahi's religious convictions by (1) physically denying his opportunity to pray and (2) having a female interrogator engage in close physical contact while playing music to induce stress since Slahi believed that Islam made music forbidden.[99] The human heart instinctively flees from God during sin—as evidenced by Adam and Eve in the garden. And the human heart instinctively knows that sin may cause God to flee from the sinner.[100] Humans are the only

[96] Hoekema, *Created in God's Image*, 76.

[97] Augustine, *Confessions* (New York: Barnes & Noble Classics, 2007), 3.

[98] Isa. 59:1–3.

[99] U.S. Senate Armed Services Committee, Inquiry into the treatment of Detainees in U.S. Custody, 136 (Nov 20, 2008), http://www.armed-services.senate.gov/imo/media/doc/Detainee-Report-Final_April-22-2009.pdf.

[100] Isa. 59:1–3.

praying animals.[101] To restrain prayer or to frustrate the urge to pray is to tear down the *Imago Dei* in the detainee and cause great spiritual distress.

Another way people try to approach God for strength is through sacred writings that they believe reveal God and his character to His people.[102] Secretary Rumsfeld's approval of removing religious items from detainees,[103] such as Korans, were acts that denied detainees the ability to approach their god. This book does not argue that the Koran reveals God.[104] This book argues that detainees use sacred writings to fulfill the desire that their Creator placed in their hearts—to glorify God and to enjoy him forever.[105] They are fulfilling that God-given desire even when their fallen heart is misdirected towards a false god. To try to break a detainee's will by frustrating his attempt to fulfill that God-given desire—the desire to find God—is to attack and deny the *Imago Dei* in him.

Extreme Assaults on Reason

Reason—the ability to think logically—is one of the most apparent distinctions between people and animals.[106] In Slahi's case, the interrogators' combined use of sleep deprivation, sensory deprivation, and physical isolation from other detainees for 48 of 54 days had the cumulative effect of driving Slahi into madness as he was observed crouching in the corner talking to people who were not there.[107] The

[101] Robert Jenson, *Systematic Theology*, vol. 2 (New York: Oxford, 1999), 58–59.

[102] John 1:1.

[103] Major General Michael Dunlavey, "Counter-Resistance Strategies" (Oct. 11, 2002), http://nsarchive.gwu.edu/torturingdemocracy/documents/20021011.pdf.

[104] The Bible is the only inspired and inerrant word of God, and Jesus is the Word. John 1:1–3.

[105] WSC 1.

[106] Grudem, *Systematic Theology*, 446.

[107] Bob Woodward, "Detainee Tortured, Says U.S. Official" *Washington Post*, Jan. 14, 2009, http://www. washingtonpost.com/wp-

destructive assault on Slahi's reason for the purpose of gaining intelligence was an assault on the *Imago Dei* in him.

Denying Human Dignity by Treating a Person as an Animal

Recognizing that God created humans in the image of God gives people "a profound sense of dignity and significance.[108] In Psalm 8, David praised God for making man his most glorious creation, crowning him like a king and giving him authority to rule over all the other creatures.

> Yet you have made him a little lower than the heavenly beings and crowned him with glory and honor. You have given him dominion over the works of your hands; you have put all things under his feet, all sheep and oxen, and also the beasts of the field, the birds of the heavens, and the fish of the sea, whatever passes along the paths of the seas.[109]

In these verses, David said that all persons have this authority and should be recognized as carrying the dignity that comes with such an office. Though all persons will occasionally conduct themselves in ways that deny such dignity,[110] Scripture requires persons to respect all human life regardless of whether the other person is behaving as the image of God.[111] In his commentary on Psalm 8, Calvin saw Scripture calling upon Christians to "remember not to consider men's evil intentions but look upon the image of God in them, which cancels and effaces their transgressions, and with its beauty and dignity allures

---

dyn/content/article/2009/01/13/AR2009011303372.html.

[108] Grudem, *Systematic Theology*, 449.

[109] Ps. 8:5–8.

[110] Rom. 3:23.

[111] J. Douma, *The Ten Commandments, trans.* Nelson D. Kloosterman. (Phillipsburg, NJ: P&R Publishing, 1996), 211.

us to love and embrace them."[112] Otherwise, treatment that denies the dignity in a person is contrary to the neighbor-love,[113] enemy-love[114] and prisoner-mercy[115] that Christ taught his followers to have.

Examples of the dehumanization of detainees are available in the political culture as well as interrogation culture. After the election of President Obama on his platform of closing the detention facility at Naval Base Guantanamo Bay, radio talk show host Rush Limbaugh attacked President Obama's concern for the issue by calling the detainees "dregs" and "human debris."[116] In separate interrogations, interrogators made Mohamedou Ould Slahi[117] and Mohammed al-Qahtani[118] wear a dog leash, led each of them around by it, and made them do dog tricks. A psychologist reportedly advised the CIA to put Abu Zubayda into a cage and treat him like an animal.[119] All of these were attempts to break detainees' wills to resist by denying them the

[112] Calvin, *Institutes*, 3.7.6.

[113] Luke 10:25–37.

[114] Matt. 5:43–45.

[115] Matthew 25:31–46 is a specific example of prisoner-mercy for Christian prisoners that is representative of the generalized good that Paul exhorts Christians in Galatians 6:10 to do for all persons inside and outside of the household of faith.

[116] Rush Limbaugh said on his broadcast: "But, look, let's talk about Gitmo for just a second because Obama does want to close it, and there are 250 really bad, bad guys at Club Gitmo. I mean these are the bottom of the barrel dregs. These are genuine human debris that are at Club Gitmo. The Democrats want to get them out of there and bring them to the United States for trial in the U.S. court system, giving them full access to constitutional rights...Now, let's take this a little step further. Let's go to the actual trial. Bring in one of these shreds of human debris...." Rush Limbaugh, "Barack Obama: Too Big To Fail," Nov. 12, 2008, http://www.rushlimbaugh.com/daily/2008/11/12/barack_obama_too_big_to_fail3.

[117] Lieutenant General Randall Schmidt and Brigadier General John Furlow, "Investigation into FBI Allegations of Detainee Abuse at Guantanamo Bay, Cuba Detention Facility," (June 9, 2005), 19–20, http://nsarchive.gwu.edu/ torturingdemocracy/documents/20050400.pdf.

[118] Woodward, "Detainee Tortured, Says U.S. Official."

[119] Jeffreys, *Spirituality and the Ethics of Torture*, 74.

dignity that the psalmist David indicated all persons have been given. The state does not have the authority to do that for interrogational purposes.

Honor the Imago Dei

Recognizing the *Imago Dei* in people should cause us to honor them and love them in sacrificial ways.[120] With regard for detainees, this does not mean releasing them from a just wartime detention that removed them from the battlefield where they were fighting an unjust war. It does mean treating the detainee with humanity and compassion while detained. It means not conceiving of them as an object or a dehumanized source of intelligence that brings the state security or the interrogator a sense of mission accomplishment when the person's will breaks. Inhumane conceptions can lead to inhumane treatment.

Regarding interrogational torture, Dietrich Bonhoeffer wrote that we misuse and dishonor the human body that God made when we use "the infliction of pain" from the interrogators position of "superiority of strength" for the purpose of "extorting . . . some desired admission or statement."[121] Instead, Scripture and the just war tradition call upon captors and interrogators to see the reflection of the *Imago Dei* in the detainee.

The Old and New Testaments teach that God will judge nations and individuals on their failures to recognize the *Imago Dei* in their enemies and prisoners among others. In Amos 1:11–12, God announced his judgment and punishment on the entire nation of Edom because their soldiers failed to show compassion and pity in war.[122] And in Matthew 25:31–46, Jesus said that when the Son of Man returns, the final judgment will consider how each individual recognized the Image of Christ in the Christian prisoner. The author of

[120] Hoekema, *Created in God's Image*, 45.
[121] Bonhoeffer, *Ethics*, 183.
[122] Amos 1:11–12.

Matthew invites everyone to consider their lives in relation to that truth.

The *Imago Dei* in the Christian

The promise of the Gospel is union with Christ and the beginning of the restoration of the uncorrupted *Imago Dei* that was lost in Adam's fall.[123] The restoration process begins with the regeneration of the heart, which is a work of the Holy Spirit[124] that enables a person to accept the teachings of Scripture and to serve God.[125] The Christian is "born again"[126] and receives a new heart and a new nature that "is being renewed in knowledge after the image of its creator."[127] Regeneration leads to sanctification, in which Christians progressively grow, through the continuing work of the Holy Spirit,[128] in their ability to participate in the righteous works that God has prepared in advance for them to do.[129] Christians are called upon not to be conformed to their former passions[130] but to be conformed to the image of Christ[131] who is the image of the Invisible God.[132] And as the Christian progressively grows in the knowledge of God and His Word, the Christian begins to think God's thoughts[133] and love with a heart like God's heart (e.g., neighbor-love,[134] enemy-love[135] and prisoner-love[136]).

[123] Col. 3:3 and 3:10.
[124] Eph. 2:4–5.
[125] Hoekema, *Created in God's Image*, 86.
[126] John 3:3, 1 Peter 1:3, Hoekema, *Created in God's Image*, 86.
[127] 2 Cor. 3:18.
[128] Phil. 2:13; 4:13.
[129] Eph. 2:10.
[130] 1 Peter 1:14.
[131] Rom. 8:29.
[132] Col. 1:15.
[133] Grudem, *Systematic Theology*, 445.
[134] Luke:10:25–37.
[135] Matt. 5:43–45.
[136] Matt. 25:31–46.

The *Imago Dei* in a Christian is not the limited list of characteristics above or any other list of characteristics provided by other theologians. The decisive aspect of the *Imago Dei* in a Christian is "the idea of Christian love" which can only be defined by Christ Jesus[137] and his love and obedience to God and love and service to neighbor.[138] G. C. Berkouwer expressed the seriousness of failing to be conformed to the image of Christ and his love when he wrote that it is not sufficient for a person to express a love for Christ and fail to act with love in the midst of others.[139] Berkouwer pointed towards the Book of 1 John, which calls upon Christians to treat others with love because Christ loved them and laid down his life for them.

> We know that we have passed out of death into life, because we love the brothers. Whoever does not love abides in death. Everyone who hates his brother is a murderer, and you know that no murderer has eternal life abiding in him. By this we know love, that he laid down his life for us, and we ought to lay down our lives for the brothers. But if anyone has the world's goods and sees his brother in need, yet closes his heart against him, how does God's love abide in him? Little children, let us not love in word or talk but in deed and in truth.[140]

The Christian who fails to act in love is denying the eschatological purpose for which Christ died and was raised from the dead.[141] The Christian is freed from fear and sin. The Christian is freed to serve God by doing righteous works of love and justice. This book argues that a Christian's use of pain, sexual exploitation, religious exploita-

[137] Paul Ramsey, *Basic Christian Ethics* (Louisville, KY: Westminster John Knox Press, 1950), 278 citing Col. 1:15.

[138] Ibid., 259.

[139] Berkouwer, *Man: The Image of God*, 116.

[140] 1 John 3:14–18.

[141] Rom. 6:1–14.

tion, extreme assaults on a person's ability to reason, and treating a person like an animal are inconsistent with the Image of Christ in the Christian.

Conclusion

For Christian policy makers involved in national security and members of the military, Scripture calls upon them to treat enemies and detainees as the *Imago Dei* or risk acting contrary to their new, redeemed nature. God has ordained that they be his vice-regents over the detainees who are in their charge. They may use force to detain soldiers and terrorists from the battlefield, and they may interrogate the prisoners. But wrestling with Scripture and the just war tradition should lead Christians to find that the following interrogation measures are *mala in se* and should never be used for any purpose: (1) the use of pain and physical abuse, (2) the use of nakedness and sexual exploitation, (3) the use of religious exploitation, (4) the use of extreme sensory deprivation, sleep deprivation, and isolation to the point it assaults the detainees ability to reason, and (5) the denial of human dignity. These techniques attempt to break the detainees will to resist by assaulting the *Imago Dei* that their creator put in them. They also deny the *Imago Dei* in the Christian who uses them or approves them.

5

What to Think about Dirty Hands and Ticking Time Bombs

And why not do evil that good may come?[1]

What shall we say then? Are we to continue in sin that grace may abound? By no means! How can we who died to sin still live in it . . . Do not present your members to sin as instruments for unrighteousness, but present yourselves to God as those who have been brought from death to life, and your members to God as instruments for righteousness.[2]

The two competing moral philosophies of modernity are deontology and utilitarianism.[3] The deontologist is a moral absolutist who chooses moral acts and would never approve of an immoral act. The utilitarian would find a choice to be moral that provides the greatest good for the greatest number of people as a consequence of the choice.[4] Just war scholars are traditionally deontological, but some just war scholars have tried to forge an ethical middle ground that justifies moral leaders taking occasional immoral actions when national

[1] Rom. 3:8.

[2] Rom. 6:1–2, 13.

[3] Jean Bethke Elshtain, "Reflections on the Problem of 'Dirty Hands,'" in *Torture: A Collection*, ed. Sanford Levinson (Oxford: Oxford University Press, 2004), 78.

[4] Elshtain, "Reflection on the Problem of Dirty Hands," 78.

security is at stake. This middle ground is symbolized by the leader with "dirty hands."[5]

Michael Walzer set the debate in his 1973 article when he described moral political leaders who must, on occasion, dirty their hands by taking immoral actions out of obligation to the responsibilities of their office.[6] For example, Walzer praises the hypothetical leader of a colony undergoing civil war who publicly opposes torture while campaigning for office but later decides to torture a captured rebel leader who knows the location of ticking time bombs hidden in apartment buildings throughout a city.[7] Walzer praises the leader's utilitarian calculation, which weighed the suffering of many people against the suffering of the rebel leader, because taking a deontological, absolutist position would have failed to live up to the duties of his office.[8] However, Walzer does not want a consistently utilitarian leader who would reason that the torture was morally good. Walzer wants the leader to accept the guilt of the immoral act because it acts as a deterrent from taking more immoral acts.[9]

This chapter will argue that Scripture and the just war tradition prohibit interrogational torture in all circumstances without exception. This book has generally argued that all detainee abuse for interrogational purposes[10] is prohibited by Scripture and the just war

[5] Michael Walzer, "Political Action: The Problem of Dirty Hands," in *Torture: A Collection*, ed. Sanford Levinson (Oxford: Oxford University Press, 2006), 61–62.

[6] Michael Walzer, "Political Action: The Problem of Dirty Hands," *Philosophy and Public Affairs* 2, 2 (Winter 1973): 160–80.

[7] Walzer, "Political Action: The Problem of Dirty Hands," 65.

[8] Ibid., 62.

[9] Ibid., 65.

[10] Chapter 4 argued that the following methods of interrogation are inconsistent with Scripture and the just war tradition: (1) the use of pain and physical abuse, (2) the use of nakedness and sexual exploitation, (3) the use of religious exploitation, (4) the use of extreme sensory deprivation, sleep deprivation, and isolation to the point it assaults the detainees ability to reason, and (5) the treatment of detainees like animals.

tradition because it violates the principles of (1) discrimination (i.e., the detainee's immunity from harm as a noncombatant who is *hors de combat*) and (2) proportionality (i.e., methods of abuse that have been deemed *mala in se* because they are an assault on the *Imago Dei* in the detainee). Torture, which falls on the far end of the spectrum of detainee abuse, would violate both of these principles.[11] James Turner Johnson has argued that discrimination is a deontological rule[12] that has no exception for situations that are *in extremis*.[13] And in the hierarchy of principles, discrimination trumps proportionality[14] in that if you cannot harm a detainee in the first place, then there is no need to conduct a balancing of the proportionality of the harm. In sum, torture as a means of warfare is "so morally repugnant"[15] to law[16] and Christ's commands for neighbor-love,[17] enemy-love[18] and prisoner-love,[19] and our own sense of what "ought not to be used"[20] that it should be determined to be *mala in se*.

Jean Bethke Elshtain, an eminent just war philosopher, demonstrates the movement of many Christians since 9/11 from a deontological position to an acceptance of dirty hands in the ticking time bomb circumstances.[21] Elshtain previously believed that torture fell into the category of "never,"[22] but that was because she had not "reflected critically" on torture. Having reconsidered Walzer's ticking

[11] James Turner Johnson, "Torture: A Just War Perspective," *The Review of Faith & International Affairs* 5, 2 (2007), 31.

[12] Ibid.

[13] James Turner Johnson, e-mail to author, 14 October 2014.

[14] Johnson, "Torture: A Just War Perspective," 31.

[15] Johnson, "Torture: A Just War Perspective," 31.

[16] Common Article 3 of the Geneva Conventions of 1949; Convention against Torture and Other Cruel, Inhuman or Degrading Treatment or Punishment.

[17] Luke:10:25–37.

[18] Matt. 5:43–45.

[19] Matt. 25:31–46.

[20] Johnson, "Torture: A Just War Perspective," 31.

[21] Elshtain, "Reflection on the Problem of Dirty Hands," 83.

[22] Ibid., 77.

time bomb scenario since the terrorist attacks of 9/11, Elshtain came to accept "torture lite,"[23] which she vaguely explains to be "moderate physical pressure."[24] Elshtain provides the following scenario:

> A bomb has been planted in an elementary school building. There are several hundred such buildings in the city in question. A known member of a terrorist gang has been apprehended. The authorities are as close to 100 percent certain as human beings can be in such circumstances that the man apprehended has specific knowledge of which school contains the deadly bomb, due to go off in an hour. He refuses to divulge the information as to which school, and officials know they cannot evacuate all of the schools . . . . It follows that some four hundred children will soon die unless the bomb is disarmed.[25]

Elshtain understands that the just war tradition is normally governed by deontological rules[26] (e.g., do not torture) but that some situations require "consequentialist considerations" because the consequences are "so serious, so dire" that the rule should be "temporarily overridden" but never changed to permit torture.[27] For a leader to refuse to override the rule would be (1) selfish "pietistic rigorism" that puts the leader's moral purity over public safety and (2) "moral laziness" that "repairs to a code rather than grappling with a terrible moral dilemma."[28]

This chapter will argue that Christians should not accept dirty hands for two reasons. First, the ticking time bomb scenario popular-

[23] Ibid., 85, citing Mark Bowden, "The Dark Art of Interrogation," *The Atlantic Monthly*, October 2003, 51–76.

[24] Elshtain, "Reflection on the Problem of Dirty Hands," 86.

[25] Ibid., 78.

[26] Ibid., 82, 87.

[27] Ibid., 87.

[28] Ibid., 88.

ized by Walzer,[29] Elshtain, and journalist Charles Krauthammer[30] are built on a limited set of facts and limited set of options that "amount to intellectual fraud."[31] Secondly, Christians such as Elshtain, Al Mohler, and Eric Patterson appear to admit and accept the sinfulness of torture yet fail to reconcile that position with their faith. This chapter concludes by arguing that Christians who accept dirty hands are being conformed to the passions of this world[32] rather than being transformed by the renewal of their minds.[33] This chapter argues that by testing these scenarios with Scripture, Christians may discern the appropriate actions that conform to the will of God for what is good and acceptable and perfect.[34]

Ticking Time Bomb Scenarios Are Intellectual Frauds

Ticking time bomb scenarios have been criticized as intellectual frauds because they (1) provide for unrealistic certainty in the factual circumstances, (2) limit the leader's options so as to only consider whether to torture or not to torture, and (3) mis-frame the entire debate over detainee treatment by developing principles based upon the most exceptional circumstances and then applying those principles to detainee treatment in general circumstances. First, regarding the factual circumstances, the scenarios provide certainty in facts that are never certain in the real world. In the scenarios, the authorities unrealistically know that there is a bomb plot, that the man they have captured is part of the plot, that not only is he part of the plot but he knows where the bomb is planted, and that there is very little time for

[29] Walzer, "Political Action: The Problem of Dirty Hands," 64–65.

[30] Charles Krauthammer, "The Truth about Torture: Its Time to be honest about doing terrible things," *Weekly Standard*, Dec. 5, 2005, http://www.weeklystandard.com/the-truth-about-torture/article/7589.

[31] David Luban, "Liberalism, Torture, and the Ticking Time Bomb," *Virginia Law Review* 94 (2005), 1425.

[32] 1 Peter 1:14.

[33] Rom. 12:2.

[34] Rom. 12:2.

other options to bear fruit. The scenario assumes that authorities have all this perfect knowledge, yet the authorities have no knowledge of where the bomb is or even where to search. Such perfect knowledge is unrealistic. In a world where Marines moving into an Iraqi town have been known to detain all military-aged-males (MAMs) out of either a suspicion that they could be the source of resistance or a desire to simply clear the streets of potential resistors, the level of suspicion necessary for detention is often less than probable cause when security or fear is the motivation. Law Enforcement fiascos like the misdirected focus of the Federal Bureau of Investigation on Richard Jewell as a suspect after the 1996 Olympic Park Bombing in Atlanta, illustrate the power of hunches to misdirect the attention of an entire nation for 88 days before Jewell was not only exonerated but later recognized as the hero for discovering the bomb.[35]

The level of fear in the environment of a ticking time bomb scenario should give a political leader pause as to the certainty of the intelligence that the authorities really have regarding the suspect that they propose to be tortured. Intelligence is more likely to be based upon hunches and degrees of likelihood rather than confidence or certainty.[36] If the suspect is responding that he doesn't know the answers to the interrogator's questions, how does the interrogator know that the person is resisting instead of actually being ignorant of the answer? The point is that the world is full of uncertainty and imperfect knowledge that can be dangerously perfected during times of fear. The ticking time bomb scenario should not be the point of reference in the discussion of detainee abuse.[37]

Second, the ticking time bomb scenario limits the political leader's options to an unrealistic dualism of whether to torture or not to

[35] Harry R. Weber, "Former Olympic Park Guard Jewell Dies" *Washington Post*, Aug. 30, 2007, http://www.washingtonpost.com/wp-dyn/content/article/2007/08/30/AR2007083000324_pf.html.

[36] Kenneth R. Himes, "The United States at War: Taking Stock" *Theological Studies* 71 (2010), 198.

[37] Luban, "Liberalism, Torture, and the Ticking Time Bomb," 1444.

torture. According to the scenario, choosing not to torture is to choose the death of many members of the public. Choosing not to torture never results in other sources of intelligence becoming available, never results in finding the bomb through other just means, and never considers the intervention of sovereign providence that might cause the bomb to malfunction and not explode. The scenario's dualism should not limit the Christian who believes in a supernatural God who is able—should he so choose—to supernaturally intervene to answer the prayers of His people and to deliver them from harm.[38]

Third, the ticking time bomb scenario mis-frames the debate onto the most controversial scenario for the deontologist to defend. David Luban believes that this is often purposeful because once the deontologist concedes that a scenario exists in which torture should be permitted, then the deontologist has admitted that the opposition to torture was not based upon principle.[39] And once the deontologist has agreed to a sell the principle, "all that is left is haggling about the price."[40]

- How many potential victims justify torturing the detainee suspect? Moral decisions should not be based upon "running the numbers."[41]
- How exceptional must the circumstances be? None of the Bush administration's uses of enhanced interrogation techniques involved a ticking time bomb. Instead, they were used to discover new terrorist plots or to gather intelligence on terrorist organizations so that the organizations could be taken apart.[42]
- Where should the line be drawn on torture methods when the suspect resists the first techniques? Once the leaders have ac-

[38] Psalms 21, 28, and 40 provide a few of the many examples.
[39] Luban, "Liberalism, Torture, and the Ticking Time Bomb," 1440.
[40] Ibid.
[41] Ibid., 1442.
[42] Ibid., 1442.

cepted the utilitarian argument that the consequences justify some torture, how can the leaders justify drawing a line on the harshness of the torture?[43]

- How can interrogators who have come to live in a torture culture judge when a line has been crossed? This is arguably exactly what happened to al-Qahtani where Secretary Rumsfeld approved certain enhanced interrogation techniques on the argument that they were coercive yet did not amount to torture when viewed individually; but, when interrogators combined them all together over an extended period of time, the sheer force of the assembled parts reduced al-Qahtani to such madness and physical deterioration that even President Bush's appointee to be the Convening Authority for the military commissions had to admit, "We tortured [al Qahtani]."[44]

While many like evangelical Al Mohler can accept torture in some exceptional circumstances while decrying it in more frequently occurring circumstances like Abu Ghraib,[45] Luban argues that Abu Ghraib is the "fully predictable image" of what results from a culture that has come to generally accept that torture can sometimes be justified.[46] We cannot reasonably expect political leaders or interrogators in a torture culture to be the "fastidious and well-meaning torturers" that the ticking time bomb scenario provides.[47]

Alberto Mora, President Bush's General Counsel to the U.S. Navy, who spoke out against DoD's use of enhanced interrogation

[43] Ibid., 1446.

[44] Bob Woodward, "Detainee Tortured, Says U.S. Official" *Washington Post*, Jan. 14, 2009, http://www. washingtonpost.com/wp-dyn/content/article/2009/01/13/AR2009011303372.html.

[45] R. Albert Mohler, "Albert Mohler on Torture," *First Things* (Jan. 6, 2010), http://www.firstthings.com/blogs/ firstthoughts/2010/01/albert-mohler-on-torture.

[46] Luban, "Liberalism, Torture, and the Ticking Time Bomb," 1452.

[47] Ibid.

techniques, recently argued at Georgetown University that the debate between torture and cruelty (e.g., torture lite) is a legal distinction without a moral difference.

> The controversy should not be only about whether we tortured, it should be about whether we inflicted cruelty. In the debate on detainee treatment we have focused too much on torture and not enough on cruelty, thus failing to bring enough moral attention to abuse that we should consider as reprehensible as torture. Fidelity to human rights principles and our existing laws requires that the application of all pain—not only severe pain—be prohibited.[48]

The ticking time bomb scenario has mis-framed the debate by focusing the attention of scholars and the public onto torture and taking the attention off of lower levels of cruelty and their unintended consequences such as any use of pain.[49]

Elshtain, Mohler, and Patterson Fail to Account for the Sin That Dirties Hands

As Christian theologians, Elshtain and evangelical Albert Mohler have difficulty accounting for sin in the ticking time bomb scenario, which both of them acknowledge in the dirty hands scenario. Recall that Walzer, who started the scenario in 1973, preferred having leaders that had a deontological code vice a utilitarian code, but were willing to depart from a deontological position in extreme

[48] Alberto Mora, "William V. O'Brien Lecture in International Law and Morality," (lecture, Georgetown University, April 30, 2013) http://anthonyclarkarend.com/humanrights/complete-text-alberto-mora-discussing-torture-and-cruel-and-inhuman-treatment-of-detainees-in-georgetowns-william-v-obrien-lecture-in-international-law-and-morality/.

[49] Mora, "William V. O'Brien Lecture in International Law and Morality."

circumstances to protect the public. Walzer liked that a deontological leader would accept the consequential guilt of torture and accounted for it through a punishment or penance that fits the crime. Elshtain accounts for the sin by arguing that the Christian is able to seek forgiveness for the use of torture, but her premeditated decision to torture and subsequently seek forgiveness lacks the moral integrity of a repentant heart[50] by continuing in the determination to torture again in the same scenario.[51] Elshtain's portrait of grace looks like a license to torture.

Mohler's essay, on the other hand, expressly accepts torture as sin without any mention of forgiveness, like Elshtain, or penance, like Walzer. Mohler, who is President of the Southern Baptist Theological Seminary, believes that Christians fighting terrorism "will inevitably look down and find dirty hands, even in doing what we would all agree is a lamentable necessity."[52] Mohler argues that the Christian soldier and interrogator "cannot privilege his desire to be free from the sin" by avoiding the sin of torture. Mohler accepts that one soldier killing another soldier on the battlefield is "generally speaking, sin,"[53] which shows that he is outside the just war camp in which Paul Ramsey,[54] Jean Bethke Elshtain,[55] Michael Walzer,[56] Daryl Charles,[57] and Darrell Cole[58] hold to the position that soldiers fighting a just war may kill the unjust aggressor without sinning. Mohler's position cannot be a just war position because it fails to accept the principle of

[50] Acts 8:22.

[51] Elshtain, "Reflection on the Problem of Dirty Hands," 83.

[52] Mohler, "Albert Mohler on Torture."

[53] Ibid.

[54] Ramsey, *The Just War*, 143.

[55] Elshtain, "Reflection on the Problem of Dirty Hands," 81.

[56] Walzer, "Political Action: The Problem of Dirty Hands," 74n6.

[57] Charles, *Between Pacifism and Jihad: Just War and Christian Tradition*, 135–36.

[58] Darrell Cole, "Darrell Cole on Torture," *First Things* (Jan. 6, 2010), http://www.firstthings.com/blogs/first thoughts/2010/01/darrell-cole-on-torture.

discrimination, which is based upon the Christian teaching on neighbor-love, and its twin-born justification and limitation on the use of force.[59]

By accepting that killing during a just war is sin while at the same time accepting the killing as a "lamentable necessity," Mohler shows that he is a Niebuhrian realist. Both the pacifist and the realist accept the understanding of the Sermon on the Mount as a "pure ethic of love and nonviolence."[60] As such, the pacifist rejects killing out of a religious conviction, but the realist concludes "that the perfect morality modeled by Jesus (and expected of his disciples) is not practical in human society and thus must be moderated by a pragmatic or realistic ethic of responsibility that requires a choice of lesser or necessary evils on behalf of the community."[61]

So starting from a flawed understanding of the soldier as sinning by merely participating in the just war, Mohler is able to equate the torture of detainees with the killing of combatants since he views both as sin. Without deontological rules like discrimination, Mohler is free to compare the use of torture in saving a life with the breaking of a speed limit in reaching a hospital and save a life.[62] Neither action is *mala in se* but *mala in situ* or bad in the situation.[63] Without a rule like discrimination, justifying the use of force against enemy aggressors and limiting the use of force against defenseless prisoners, Mohler has no justification or limitation to offer Christians who are engaged in national security and trying to discern God's will for what is right and perfect.[64] His recommendation is to accept the "lamentable necessity."

[59] Ramsey, *The Just War*, 144.

[60] Keith Pavlischek, "Reinhold Niebuhr, Christian Realism, and Just War Theory: A Critique," in *Christianity and Power Politics Today*, ed. Eric Patterson (New York: Palgrave Macmillan, 2008), 55.

[61] Ibid.

[62] Mohler, "Albert Mohler on Torture."

[63] Ibid.

[64] Rom. 12:2.

Eric Patterson, Dean of Regent University's Robertson School of Government, follows Mohler's same logic.[65] While the just war tradition holds that the principle of discrimination trumps the principle of proportionality when the two come into conflict,[66] Patterson argues that this should change and that proportionality should trump discrimination because "Times have changed and it is appropriate to reconsider how decision makers and war fighters should prosecute conflicts in the twenty-first century."[67] But rather than subordinate discrimination, Patterson implicitly rejects it when he fails to employ it in his review of the ticking time bomb scenario.[68] In the case of a nuclear device in London or Tokyo, Patterson simply finds that "torture is proportionate to the threat" and that authorities may "rightly stop at nothing to extract the necessary information about its whereabouts."[69] To recognize no limit to torture is not the "torture lite" of Elshtain or the enhanced interrogation techniques approved by Secretary Rumsfeld, since it leaves the door open to electric prods and the chopping of fingers.

Patterson is unable to articulate whether torture is sinful or righteous. Patterson quizzically calls the unlimited use of torture to be "rightly" employed in the ticking time bomb scenario yet in the same paragraph calls it the "lesser evil" than the deaths of thousands. It cannot be both. To call it "rightly" is to take a purely utilitarian position that engages in the balancing test and then calls the action moral. To call it a "lesser evil" is to follow Walzer's camp within the just war tradition that engages in the utilitarian balancing test but doesn't call the action moral, without accepting the guilt and seeking forgiveness (e.g., Elshtain) or doing penance (e.g., Walzer). The third

[65] Eric Patterson, *Just War Thinking: Morality and Pragmatism in the Struggle agaisnt Contemporary Threats* (Lanham, MD: Lexongton Books, 2007), 66.

[66] Johnson, e-mail to author.

[67] Patterson, *Just War Thinking*, 75.

[68] Ibid., 66.

[69] Ibid.

position is the historic just war position that discrimination is a deontological rule and that torture is a *mala in se* and not *mala in situ*.[70] Patterson intends to be in the just war tradition, but his articulation of the ticking time bomb scenario accepts evil and calls it right.

Finally, returning to Elshtain, it is regrettable that she defended her intellectual evolution towards accepting dirty hands in extreme situations by attacking those who have not evolved or abandoned the deontological position for any circumstance. Elshtain argued that a deontological leader selfishly ranks "his or her 'purity' above human lives,"[71] "becomes directly complicit in the deaths of hundreds of innocents,"[72] lapses "into pietistic rigorism in which one's own moral purity is ranked above other goods,"[73] and engages in "moral laziness [when a leader] repairs to a code rather than grappling with a terrible moral dilemma."[74] Mohler similarly used *ad hominem* rhetoric, arguing, "Moral cowards duck these questions even as the morally unserious dismiss them."[75] Mohler insisted that Christians "cannot deny that there could exist circumstances in which such uses of torture might be necessary."[76] Elshtain and Mohler fail to acknowledge that thoughtful Christians might take the deontological position out fear of God and the belief that Christ calls his followers to identify the detainee with the *Imago Dei* and treat him accordingly. Instead, Elshtain and Mohler attacked through mischaracterization. Elshtain to the greater extent, yet Mohler as well, failed to show grace towards Christians who might consider themselves in union with Christ and have a desire to engage in righteousness conduct.

70 Johnson, e-mail to the author.

71 Elshtain, "Reflection on the Problem of Dirty Hands," 83.

72 Ibid.

73 Ibid., 87–88.

74 Ibid., 88.

75 Mohler, "Albert Mohler on Torture."

76 Ibid.

Conclusion: Christian Leaders Should Reject Dirty Hands

Christian leaders must consider whether to be conformed to Christ or to the passions and fears of the world. In 1 Peter 1, the Apostle Peter calls upon Christians not to be conformed to the passions of the world but to "be holy in all your conduct, since it is written, 'You shall be holy, for I am holy.'"[77] Scripture teaches that Christ was holy and that there was no sin in Him.[78] So as the Christian is in union with a Holy Christ,[79] Christians should strive to adopt political, philosophical, and theological positions that do not purposefully intend to engage in sin in advance of a situation. To admit to the intent of dirty hands in advance of a ticking time bomb scenario appears to accept the sinful option. Elshtain is right that a Christian leader who tortures or approves of torture may find forgiveness, and the Christian should seek it, but this section argues that the Christian should not continue to live with an intent to take the same action again in a similar scenario.[80] When the Apostle Paul asks, "Are we to continue in sin that grace may abound?"[81] He answers, "By no means! How can we who died to sin still live in it?"[82] Again, Paul asks, "Are we to sin because we are not under law but under grace?"[83] And again Paul answers, "By no means! Do you not know that if you present yourselves to anyone as obedient slaves, you are slaves of the one whom you obey, either of sin, which leads to death, or of obedience, which leads to righteousness."

Christian leaders should reject dirty hands. They should follow the leadership of King Hezekiah of Judah and not King Ahaz of Israel. Both kings faced enemies that possessed overwhelming power.

[77] 1 Peter 1:13–16.
[78] John 1:5.
[79] Rom. 6:1–14.
[80] 1 John 1:6–2:2.
[81] Rom. 6:1.
[82] Rom. 6:2.
[83] Rom. 6:15.

Regarding King Ahaz of Israel, the prophet Isaiah challenged him not to fear the enemy but to trust in the Lord to deliver Israel.[84] Ahaz replied, "I will not put the Lord to the test,"[85] and he sought a political solution in which he formed an alliance with Tiglath-Pileser and the ungodly Assyrian Empire.[86] Assyria responded quickly and stopped the threat, but subjugated Israel in the process and set in motion a relationship that ended in the destruction of Israel and the exile of her people.[87]

Regarding King Hezekiah of Judah, Sennacherib and the Assyrians marched into Judah and besieged Jerusalem, trapping King Hezekiah inside. Hezekiah refused to surrender and seek a political solution with Sennacherib, praying and trusting the Lord to deliver Judah.[88] That night the angel of the Lord went out and struck down 185,000 Assyrians in the camp, and Sennacherib had to depart and return to Nineveh where he was killed by his sons while worshipping his gods.[89] This book does not argue that Christian leaders should trust in the Lord and wait for the angel of the Lord to come without taking action—Hezekiah had taken action, preparing Judah to defend itself during a long siege. Instead, this book argues that Christian leaders should take righteous actions to fight wars and terrorism while rejecting evil and while hoping that the Lord may choose to bless their righteous and just actions with effectiveness.

In regards to the ticking time bomb scenario, the Christian is not faced with a Hobbesian choice of either employing torture or seeing thousands die. Leaders must reject the sin of torture and ask the Lord to bless efforts to evacuate the locations concerned, pursue all intelligence leads with righteous methods, search for the bomb, and pray

[84] Willem A. VanGemeren, *Interpreting the Prophetic Word* (Grand Rapids: Zondervan, 1990), 250.

[85] Isa. 7:12.

[86] 2 Kings 16:7.

[87] VanGemeren, *Interpreting the Prophetic Word*, 250.

[88] 2 Kings 19:19.

[89] 2 Kings 19:35–37.

that the terrorist's bomb may malfunction and fail like Richard Reid's failed shoe bombing on American Airlines flight 63 in 2001;[90] Umar Farouk Abdulmutallab's failed underwear bombing of Northwest Airlines flight 253 in 2009,[91] or Faisal Shahzad's failed car bombing of Times Square in 2010.[92] These are all options not presented by the ticking time bomb scenario. Christian leaders must act with appropriate concern for national security, but they should not act out of the fear that is a driving passion in the world.

Christian theologians and philosophers should oppose the assumptions of the ticking time bomb scenario and put their faith in the providence of a God who is able to deliver the righteous through the lawful and just means employed by His people such as just forms of interrogations.[93] They should also refuse to follow utilitarian models of moral reasoning that base their decisions solely upon the consequences that will result. Theologians should uphold the just war tradition's deontological principle of discrimination and refuse to engage in methods that are *mala in se* because they attack the *Imago Dei* in the detainee.

[90] William Branigin, "Man Charged with Plotting Shoe Bomb Attack," *Washington Post*, Oct. 4, 2004, http://www.washingtonpost.com/wp-dyn/articles/A6218-2004Oct4.html.

[91] Josh Meyer and Peter Nicholas, "Obama calls jet incident a 'serious reminder,'" *Los Angeles Times*, Dec. 29, 2009, http://articles.latimes.com/2009/dec/29/nation/la-na-plane-terror29-2009dec29.

[92] Jerry Markon and Spencer S. Hsu, "Probe in failed Times Square attack focusing on Pakistani Taliban," *Washington Post*, May 5, 2010, http://www.washingtonpost.com/wp-dyn/content/article/2010/05/04/AR2010050400192.html.

[93] Ps. 40.

6

The Problem with Clean Hands and Using Scripture to Justify the Use of Pain During Interrogations

[T]he commander ordered that Paul be taken into the barracks. He directed that he be flogged and interrogated in order to find out why the people were shouting at him like this. 25 As they stretched him out to flog him, Paul said to the centurion standing there, "Is it legal for you to flog a Roman citizen who hasn't even been found guilty?"[1]

Torture of the body is to be distinguished from corporal punishment....It is also to be distinguished from retributive punishment.[2]

Two evangelical Christian theologians who argue that Scripture warrants the state's infliction of "substantial pain"[3] or "significant pain"[4] during interrogations are seminary professors Wayne Grudem and John Jefferson Davis. Davis limits his argument to the ticking time bomb scenario, but Grudem applies his argument to the interro-

[1] Acts 22:24–25 (NIV).

[2] Bonhoeffer, *Ethics*, trans. Neville Horton Smith (New York: Simon & Schuster, 1995), 183.

[3] John Jefferson Davis, "John Jefferson Davis on Torture," *First Things* (Jan 10, 2010), http://www.firstthings.com/blogs/firstthoughts/2010/01/john-jefferson-davis-on-torture; Wayne Grudem, *Politics According to the Bible* (Grand Rapids: Zondervan, 2010).

[4] Grudem, *Politics According to the Bible*, 430.

gation of any detained terrorist. Both men base their arguments on Romans 13:3–4,[5] which has been traditionally understood as the authority for the state to exercise capital *punishment*[6] as well as lesser *punishments* for wrongdoing.[7] Grudem additionally rests the state's authority on Proverbs 13:24,[8] which has been traditionally understood as authority for parents to use corporal *punishment* as part of the discipline and instruction of their children.[9] Thoughtful Christians looking for theological rigor from two very accomplished theologians will find that these two essays are not characteristic of their other works. Grudem and Davis cite Scripture for an unusual proposition and do not provide any authorities that agree with their position on these Scriptures. Nonetheless, this author respects the men enough to deal with their arguments for expanding the scope of the sword and the rod from instruments authorized for punishment purposes to include interrogational purposes.

This chapter will argue that Grudem and Davis (1) fail to make a persuasive case that Scripture justifies the use of pain for the purpose of seeking information and (2) fail to establish authoritative limits in law or Scripture for the use of pain. This chapter will also demonstrate that Grudem mishandles the law and the just war tradition in his strident advocacy of his position on the use of pain. Lastly, this chapter will conclude that these works are not a service to those Christians who will accept the Scriptural warrant to employ interrogational pain on behalf of the state and then—intentionally or uninten-

[5] Davis, "John Jefferson Davis on Torture"; Grudem, *Politics According to the Bible*, 425–33.

[6] James D. G. Dunn, *Romans 9–16*, vol. 38b (Dallas: Word Books, 1988), 764; C.K. Barrett, *A Commentary on the Espistle to the Romans*, (London: A & C Black, 1991), 227.

[7] John Murray, *The Epistle to the Romans*, vol. 2, (Grand Rapids: Wm. B. Eerdmans, 1965), 153.

[8] Grudem, *Politics According to the Bible*, 430.

[9] Bruce Waltke, *The Book of Proverbs: Chapters 1–15* (Grand Rapids: William B. Eerdmans Publishing, 2004), 574 Derek Kidner, *Proverbs* (Downers Grove, IL: InterVarsity Press, 2008), 99–100.

tionally—disregard Grudem's vague limits on the use of pain because they are untethered from any foundation in Scripture or law. The nation's experience between 2002 and 2006 should give all Christians pause as to how fallen people will act when the law is removed as a limit and the executive replaces it with a policy of humane treatment.[10]

Failing to Make a Scriptural Case for Pain

Grudem and Davis fail to make a persuasive case for the use of pain as a method of interrogation because there are two reasons that Scripture cannot support it. First, the scope of the sword's authority in Romans 13 is limited to punishments and cannot be expanded to interrogations. Secondly, the rod's authority in the verses that Grudem cites is limited to a parent's purpose in imposing punishment and instruction on their child and cannot be extended to state purposed interrogation.

The Sword of Romans 13 is Not the Whip of Acts 22

Grudem and Davis both argue that Romans 13:3–4 provide states with not only the authority to punish convicted criminals, but they make the novel argument that this passage provides authority to use pain in seeking information. Neither theologian deals with Acts 22:22–30 and the Roman tribune's limited authority that did not extend to interrogation. When the Roman tribune finds out that the Apostle Paul is a Roman citizen, he rescinds his order that the Paul "should be examined by flogging, to find out" what crime he had committed.[11] That is the same Paul who wrote about the ruler's power to bear the sword in Romans 13:3–4. This raises two serious questions

[10] George W. Bush, Memo, "Humane Treatment of Taliban and al Qaeda Detainees" (Feb. 7, 2002), 1,
http://nsarchive.gwu.edu/NSAEBB/NSAEBB127/02.02.07.pdf.

[11] Acts 22:25.

that Grudem and Davis neglect: (1) how much authority does the sword symbolize and (2) who is the wrongdoer in Romans 13:4?

As demonstrated by the Roman tribune's "fear" as well as that of the Roman interrogators who "withdrew from him immediately,"[12] the first recipients of Paul's epistle to the Romans would have only understood the sword in Romans 13:3–4 to represent the ruler's "penal prerogative"[13] to punish those who have been found guilty, which is a wholly different context from the Roman whip of interrogational torture. Interrogation by its nature is used for the purpose of gathering information—not punishment. James D. G. Dunn believed that the sword could not have been a symbol of pre-trial corporal punishment to Paul's Roman readers since they "had the right of appeal to a higher court and as far as the emperor."[14] Accordingly, in the prisoner context, the wrongdoer could only be a person who has been found guilty of wrongdoing and received a punishment from a lawful authority such as a judge. That is a completely different context than Acts 22:22–30, and neither Grudem nor Davis is able to support the link.

Spare the Rod, Spoil the . . . Terrorist?

Grudem inappropriately equates the use of pain in seeking information from a prisoner to the biblically legitimate authority for parents to use corporal punishment as part of instructing their child.[15] Grudem primarily cites Proverbs 13:24 but includes four other verses which strictly apply to the context of parental discipline. Grudem expounds on these verses with his personal experience punishing his children by "squeezing the trapezius muscle that runs between the shoulder and the neck."[16] Of this practice, Grudem writes, "It hurts!"[17]

[12] Acts 22:29.

[13] Murray, *The Epistle to the Romans*, 153.

[14] Dunn, *Romans 9–16*, 764 citing Acts 25:11.

[15] Grudem, *Politics According to the Bible*, 430.

[16] Ibid. Grudem also cites Proverbs 22:15 ("Folly is bound up in the heart of a child..."), 23:13–14 ("Do not withhold discipline from a child ...you will

Grudem analogizes his parental discipline to the state's interrogation practice and argues that interrogators may biblically "inflict even acute pain" so long as it does not leave "lasting physical damage,"[18] which implies biblical warrant for temporary physical damage as well as lasting mental damage.

Proverbs 13:24 cannot provide authority for the state's infliction of pain during interrogation. The use of parental force in that verse and the other four that Grudem cites are based in the "Lord's pedagogic motive" for parents to have in punishing children.[19] Interrogation is neither punishment nor pedagogic. The detainee suspected of terrorism is not the interrogator's child. The interrogator does not love the detainee like his own child. The interrogator's purpose is not to teach the terrorist in "the school of wisdom"[20] as parents teach their children. The detainee is a defenseless prisoner under the domination of his captor while the parent disciplines "those he loves best"[21] inside a covenantal relationship that provides natural limitations on the use of force. Finally, the interrogator is motivated to use pain in order to save the state while the parent is motivated to save the child from insolence, laziness, folly, the whore's deep pit, and eternal death.[22] Grudem's comparison is not justified.

Dietrich Bonhoeffer wrote in stark opposition to Grudem's argument. "Torture of the body is to be distinguished from the corporal chastisement of which the purpose is to educate the mentally immature to a state of independence."[23] Bonhoeffer finds other marks of distinction between torture and corporal punishment in that torture is

---

save his soul from Sheol"), and 29:15 ("The rod and reproof give wisdom, but a child left to himself brings shame to his mother") as scriptural authority for the use of pain during detainee interrogations.

[17] Grudem, *Politics According to the Bible*, 430.

[18] Ibid.

[19] Waltke, *The Book of Proverbs Chapters 1–15*, 574.

[20] Kidner, *Proverbs*, 144.

[21] Ibid.

[22] Waltke, *The Book of Proverbs Chapters 15–31*, 216.

[23] Bonhoeffer, *Ethics*, 183.

more arbitrary and brutal in its practice and by its purpose seeks a different outcome such as a statement. His argument reasons that corporal punishment seeks to restore the relationship between the parent and child while "any torture inflicts the most extreme dishonour on the human being, and consequently engenders an intense hatred" that will seek to "avenge itself" against the tormentor.[24]

Failing to Provide Authoritative Limits on the Use of Pain

Although Grudem provides Scripture to justify the use of pain, he provides no authority in Scripture or law that would limit the use of pain. Instead, Grudem advocates stripping away the primary law that affords protection to detainees (i.e., Common Article 3 of the Geneva Conventions). In its place, Grudem provides the following five limits: that a government should never be allowed to commit immoral acts, deny medical treatment, carry out sadistic exploitation, force a prisoner to violate a religious conviction, or engage in action that would shock the conscience.[25] The problem with this list is that Grudem does not provide any authority in Scripture or law for these limits. They are his and any reader may disregard them without consequence. As a theologian writing a book titled, "Politics According to the Bible: A Comprehensive Resource for Understanding Modern Political Issues in Light of Scripture," Grudem would be more balanced and helpful if he provided as much Scriptural justification for his limits on the use of pain as he does his warrant for the use of pain.

Grudem Mishandles the Law of War

In arguing for the stripping away of the Geneva Conventions, Grudem misstates the law of war. Grudem begins his argument by examining the legal position of POWs and praising the policy of

[24] Ibid.
[25] Grudem, *Politics According to the Bible*, 429.

humane treatment in the Third Geneva Convention[26] by equating it with Jesus' command to "love your neighbor."[27] Then Grudem shifts to terrorists and argues that they are an exception to that policy.[28] Grudem uses italics to stridently argue that "according to international law, *he is not entitled to the protections of the Geneva Conventions.*"[29] That is a misstatement of the law as determined by the U.S. Supreme Court,[30] the International Court of Justice,[31] and the International Criminal Tribunal for the former Yugoslavia.[32] It also contradicts Department of Defense Directive 2310.01E, which states that military service members shall "observe the requirements of the law of war and shall apply, without regard to a detainee's legal status, at a minimum the standards articulated in Common Article 3 to the Geneva Conventions of 1949."[33] Despite publishing his book seven years after the U.S. Supreme Court's ruling in *Hamdan v. Rumsfeld*, in which the Court held that Common Article 3 affords protections for all persons detained on the battlefield,[34] as well as seven years after the publication of DoD Directive 2310.01E, Grudem neither makes any mention of these contrary positions nor gives readers notice that he is

[26] Ibid., 425.

[27] Ibid., 427 citing Matthew 5:44.

[28] By arguing that detainees are "exceptions" to the policy that Grudem equated with Jesus' command to love your neighbor in Matthew 5:44, Grudem makes the strong implication that detainees are an exception to Jesus' command to love enemies. This is a startling argument for which Grudem provides no support. Grudem, *Politics According to the Bible*, 428.

[29] Ibid., 428 (italics in the original).

[30] Hamdan v. Rumsfeld, 548 U.S. 557, 736 (2006).

[31] Nicaragua v. United States, 1986 International Court of Justice 14, 218, 25 I.L.M. 1023.

[32] Prosecutor v. Tadic, Case No. IT-94-1, Decision on the Defence Motion for Interlocutory Appeal on Jurisdiction, 102 (International Criminal Tribunal for the former Yugoslavia Appellate Chamber, Oct. 2, 1995).

[33] DoD Directive 2310.01E, "The Department of Defense Detainee Program" (Sept. 5, 2006).

[34] 548 U.S. 557, 736 (2006).

advocating a position that President Bush reversed soon after the *Hamdan* decision.

Grudem Mishandles the Just War Tradition

Although he argues for stripping away the law, Grudem does provide philosophical criteria to justify his five proposed limits on the interrogational use of pain.[35] Grudem quotes a list of eleven principles[36] formed by evangelical seminary professor Daniel Heimbach.[37] The problem is that the eleven *jus ad bellum* principles are appropriate in analyzing the justification for a war and are not appropriate to a *jus in bello* analysis of the justification for a method of war. A traditional just war analysis would only to apply the two *jus in bello* principles of discrimination and proportionality. While Grudem's list includes proportionality, it omits the principle of discrimination, which chapter 2 demonstrated is founded upon Christ's teaching of neighbor-love and its twin-born justification and limitation regarding methods of warfare.[38] Discrimination is the principle reflected in Common Article 3 and its requirement that all noncombatants—including detainees—be treated humanely without "violence to life and person...cruel treatment, and torture" as well as "outrages upon personal dignity, in particular humiliating and degrading treatment."[39]

Grudem and Heimbach wrongly omit the principle of discrimination as a protection for defenseless detainees. Grudem argues that prisoners who are hiding intelligence that could save "thousands of lives from terrible destruction" are still engaged in combat. Regarding why this philosophical rationale applies to a detainee and not a POW

[35] Grudem, *Politics According to the Bible*, 431.

[36] Ibid.

[37] Daniel R. Heimbach, "Daniel Heimbach on Torture," *First Things* (Jan. 6, 2010), http://www.firstthings.com/ blogs/firstthoughts/2010/01/daniel-heimbach-on-torture.

[38] Paul Ramsey, *The Just War: Force and Political Responsibility* (Lanham, MD: Rowman & Littlefield Publishers, Inc., 2002), 144.

[39] Common Article 3 of the Geneva Conventions of 1949.

(recall that Grudem praised the POW protections[40]), Grudem explains that POWs fight honorably, but this explanation fails to account for the Nazis who committed great atrocities but were still accorded POW status.[41] Grudem also does not explain why "thousands of lives" re-categorize the detainee as a combatant and not hundreds of lives or even one life. In Heimbach's address where he provided the eleven criteria, he argued that discrimination should not apply when the detainee is "serving a power threatening national security and public safety."[42] Grudem's and Heimbach's arguments contravene the long established law of war as well as re-established domestic law since 2006. They also contradict the long established principle of discrimination as a *jus in bello* criteria.[43]

Conclusion: Grudem and Davis Provide Biblical Warrant with No Biblical Limits

Grudem and Davis fail to appreciate the effect of their arguments, which would provide Scriptural justification without Scriptural limitations for the use of "substantial pain"[44] and "significant pain"[45] during interrogations. Their arguments betray their Calvinist convictions on the second use of the law, which is to restrain evil.[46] Chapter 1 demonstrated that removing the fetters of the law from wartime interrogations resulted in the use of pain; sexual exploitation; religious

[40] Grudem, *Politics According to the Bible*, 427.

[41] Darrell Cole, "Darrell Cole on Torture," *First Things* (Jan. 6, 2010), http://www.firstthings.com/blogs/first thoughts/2010/01/darrell-cole-on-torture.

[42] Daniel Heimbach, "The Problem with Assessing Torture," *Global Journal of Classic Theology* 10, 1 (undated) http://www.globaljournalct.com/wp-content/uploads/ 2014/08/Daniel_Heimbach_Torture_vol_10_ no_1.pdf.

[43] James Turner Johnson, "Torture: A Just War Perspective," *The Review of Faith & International Affairs* 5, 2 (2007): 31.

[44] Davis, "John Jefferson Davis on Torture."

[45] Grudem, *Politics According to the Bible*, 430.

[46] Calvin, *Institutes*, 2.7.10.

exploitation; the assault on reason using extreme sensory deprivation, sleep deprivation, and isolation; and the treatment of detainees like animals. Richard Mouw, a Calvinist and former President at Fuller Theological Seminary, has argued that the images of soldiers abusing and humiliating detainees at Abu Ghraib horrify him not only because of the evil in those soldiers but because of the evil that lurks in the deep places of his soul and the soul of every other person.[47] States should not remove protections based upon the dishonor of the detainee but because of the potential for dishonor in the captor.

Christian theologians should also consider the third use of the law for Christians, in which the law reveals what is pleasing to the God[48] with whom the Christian is in union. This book concurs with Grudem that The Third Geneva Convention relative to the treatment of POWs reflects Jesus' command in Matthew 5:44 to love our enemies.[49] This book has argued that Common Article 3 of the Geneva Conventions also reflects Jesus' commands for the neighbor-love,[50] enemy-love[51] and prisoner-love[52] as well as the second greatest commandment[53] and the royal law.[54] Christians should show great pause before removing laws that protect the weakest and most defenseless people in society.[55] And theologians should be as diligent in warning Christians about Scripture's limits on the use of pain as they are in advocating for Scripture's warrant for pain.

[47] Richard Mouw, "Original Sin in Abu Ghraib," *Beliefnet*, (July 23, 2009), http://www.beliefnet.com/Faiths/ Christianity/2004/05/Original-Sin-In-Abu-Ghraib.aspx?p=2.

[48] Calvin, *Institutes*, 2.7.12–13.

[49] Grudem, *Politics According to the Bible*, 427.

[50] Luke 10:25–37.

[51] Matt. 5:43–45.

[52] Matt. 25:31–46.

[53] Matt. 22:39.

[54] James 2:8.

[55] Ex. 22:21–23.

7

Thoughts about a City on a Hill

You are the light of the world. A city set on a hill cannot be hidden. Nor do people light a lamp and put it under a basket, but on a stand, and it gives light to all in the house. In the same way, let your light shine before others, so that they may see your good works and give glory to your Father who is in heaven.[1]

The Pew Forum on Religion in Public Life determined in 2009 that white evangelical Christians in the United States were in favor of "the use of torture against suspected terrorists" more than any other religious group.[2] It determined that 62% of white evangelicals would agree that torture "can often" or "can sometimes be justified" while only 51% of white Roman Catholics would, 46% of white mainline Protestants would, and only 40% of the religiously unaffiliated would.[3] When adding those who believe that torture "can rarely be justified," the survey determined that 8 in 10 white evangelicals could justify torture in some circumstance.[4] After the survey was released, a news item in the *Washington Post* observed that the internet became a

[1] Matt. 5:14–16.

[2] Pew Research, "The Religious Dimensions of the Torture Debate," *Religion & Public Life Project*, Apr. 29, 2009, http://www.pewforum.org/2009/04/29/the-religious-dimensions-of-the-torture-debate/.

[3] Ibid.

[4] Ibid.

forum for many to accuse evangelicals of "forsaking the love-thine-enemy doctrine of Christianity."[5] This and other examples of a public backlash against evangelical Christians caused Pew to re-analyze the survey, and it concluded that political party affiliation had an even more distinct affect on a person's ability to justify torture than religious affiliation. It found 64% of Republicans would agree that torture can often or sometimes be justified while only 36% of Democrats would.[6] The researchers at Pew stated, "Party and ideology are much better predictors of views on torture than are religion and most other demographic factors."[7]

Considering the Pew survey and the many Christian leaders who have provided arguments in favor of torture,[8] provided theological legitimacy for dirty hands,[9] or Scriptural legitimacy for clean hands that inflict pain,[10] this book concludes that evangelical Christians have

[5] "God in Government," *Washington Post*, May 9, 2009, *Religion & Public Life Project*, May 7, 2009, http://www.washingtonpost.com/wp-dyn/content/article/2009/05/08/AR2009050803590.html.

[6] Pew Research, "The Torture Debate: A Closer Look," *Religion & Public Life Project*, May7, 2009, http://www.pewforum.org/2009/05/07/the-torture-debate-a-closer-look/.

[7] Ibid.

[8] Chuck Colson, "Justified under Some Circumstances," *Faith Street*, Nov. 9, 2007, http://www.faithstreet.com/onfaith/2007/11/09/justified-under-some-circumsta/2968; Cal Thomas, "Torturing Ourselves to Death," *Faith Street*, Nov. 13, 2007, http://www.faithstreet.com/onfaith/2007/11/13/torturing-ourselves-to-death/1091.

[9] R. Albert Mohler, "Albert Mohler on Torture," *First Things* (Jan. 6, 2010), http://www.firstthings.com/blogs/ firstthoughts/2010/01/albert-mohler-on-torture; Eric Patterson, *Just War Thinking: Morality and Pragmatism in the Struggle agaisnt Contemporary Threats* (Lanham, MD: Lexongton Books, 2007), 66; Jean Bethke Elshtain, "Reflections on the Problem of 'Dirty Hands,'" in *Torture: A Collection*, ed. Sanford Levinson (Oxford: Oxford University Press, 2004), 83.

[10] Wayne Grudem, *Politics According to the Bible* (Grand Rapids: Zondervan, 2010), 430; John Jefferson Davis, "John Jefferson Davis on Torture," *First Things* (Jan 10, 2010), http://www.firstthings.

been shaped more by politics,[11] utilitarian modes of reasoning,[12] Christian realism,[13] and other patterns of this world than by the transforming and renewing of their mind[14] that comes from wrestling with God's word to discern the character of God and what he finds good and acceptable and perfect.[15] Al Mohler's 2500 word defense of Christians with dirty hands[16] does not provide a single Scriptural citation. Wayne Grudem's eight page discussion of the "Coercive Interrogation of Prisoners"[17] only dedicates 2 of the 37 paragraphs to an examination of Scripture in a book titled, *Politics According to the Bible: A Comprehensive Resource for Understanding Modern Political Issues in Light of Scripture.*

This book concludes that the minds and hearts of evangelical political leaders, military service members, seminary professors, pastors, and church members were not prepared to recognize and honor the *imago Dei* in the detainees captured during the global war on terrorism.[18] This is evident in chapter 1, which documented the U.S.

---

com/blogs/firstthoughts/2010/01/john-jefferson-davis-on-torture.

[11] Pew Research, "The Torture Debate: A Closer Look."

[12] Michael Walzer, "Political Action: The Problem of Dirty Hands," in *Torture: A Collection*, ed. Sanford Levinson (Oxford: Oxford University Press, 2006), 61–62; Elshtain, "Reflection on the Problem of Dirty Hands," 78–79.

[13] Mohler, "Albert Mohler on Torture."

[14] Rom. 12:12.

[15] Rom. 12:2.

[16] Mohler, "Albert Mohler on Torture."

[17] Grudem, *Politics According to the Bible*, 425.

[18] Daryl Charles has argued that evangelicals were unprepared to provide ethically thoughtful responses to general just war questions raised by the terrorist attacks of 9/11. He believes that this is due the unformed conscience of evangelicalism. Charles argues that the evangelical church has failed to articulate a rationale for a social ethic on perennial issues of public policy that is informed by Scripture and the tradition of the Church. He thinks that evangelicals are effective at personal moral formation due to an appropriate emphasis on personal salvation and preparing for life in the eternal city, but that evangelicals are neglecting to redeem the current "city" that they live in. Charles looks to the books in Christian bookstores (e.g., novels about the end times, Christian romance novels, and books teaching Christians to unlock

Government's official use of (1) pain and physical abuse, (2) sexual exploitation, (3) religious exploitation, (4) extreme sensory deprivation, sleep deprivation, and isolation to the point it assaulted a detainees ability to reason, and (5) the treatment of detainees like animals. This book has argued that wrestling with Scripture on the treatment of prisoners during war should lead Christians to reject those interrogation techniques because they violate the biblical *jus in bello* principles of discrimination and proportionality.

- Discrimination. Chapter 3 argued that discrimination is the deontological principle that requires the state to distinguish between combatants and noncombatants and justifies an attack on combatants while requiring that noncombatant prisoners be respected and protected while in detention. The state should discriminate in this way because Jesus discriminates this way, calling upon all people to recognize the *Imago Dei* in neighbors, enemies, the sick and prisoners.[19]
- Proportionality. Chapter 4 argued that proportionality is the principle that considers whether the method of warfare is proportional to the end that is being sought, and that when it is applied to the U.S. Government's interrogation techniques discussed above, Christians should reject them as *mala in se* because they assault the *Imago Dei* in the detainee as well as the Image of Christ in the Christian who approves the technique or uses the technique.

This book also argued in chapter 5 that Christians should reject the dirty hands scenario as an intellectual fraud and hold on to political

God's blessings for them) and concludes that American evangelicals are focused on themselves and the church to the exclusion of all the other buildings on the public square. J. Daryl Charles, *Between Pacifism and Jihad: Just War and Christian Tradition* (Downer's Grove, IL: InterVarsity Press, 2005), 2, 11, 173.

[19] Luke 10:25–37; Matt. 5:43–48; Matt. 25:31–46.

and theological positions that prohibit purposefully planning to sin while consciously accepting the sinfulness of the action.[20]

On almost every issue not involving national security, evangelicals have a strong record of wrestling with Scripture and faithfully applying it to their lives. Evangelicals have wrestled with the 24 verses in Psalm 139[21] and come to recognize the *Imago Dei* in the unborn child. The public record provides ample evidence that evangelicals have acted on those convictions and become strong advocates for the unborn children in their communities. This book concludes that evangelical preachers, teachers and church members should consider the U.S. treatment of detainees and then wrestle with Christ's teaching on neighbor-love,[22] enemy-love[23] and prisoner-love[24] as well as the Old Testament's teaching on love for the powerless in our society.[25] Pastors should preach and teachers should teach on the *Imago Dei*. Otherwise, evangelicals will be even more unprepared for the next war since the philosophical and theological support for the abuse of detainees and terrorists has largely gone unanswered in evangelical circles.

The Republican nominees for President in 2012 and 2016 have campaigned to allow waterboarding to remain a tool that is available for use during interrogations. That was the position of Mitt Romney in 2012.[26] And that was the position of Donald Trump in 2016, who has advocated for interrogations that are more aggressive than waterboarding. Trump has made the following statements about the treatment of terrorists:

[20] Rom. 6:1–14.

[21] Ps. 139.

[22] Luke 10:25–37.

[23] Matt. 5:43–45.

[24] Matt. 25:31–46.

[25] Ex. 22:21–23.

[26] Charlie Savage, "Election to Decide Future Interrogation Methods in Terrorism Cases," *New York Times* (Sept. 27, 2012), http://www.nytimes.com/2012/09/28/us/politics/election-will-decide-future-of-interrogation-methods-for-terrorism-suspects.html.

- "I would bring back waterboarding, and I would bring back a hell of a lot worse than waterboarding."[27]
- "They said, 'What do you think about waterboarding?' And I said, 'I like it a lot, and I don't think it's tough enough.' . . . And I have tremendous evangelical support,"[28]
- "We have to beat the savages" and "broaden" the laws to permit torture.[29]

Unless evangelical Christians who oppose waterboarding speak out and publish their opinions, then there will be no evidence that the evangelical church opposed waterboarding. The unfortunate result may be that when Christians consider the use of waterboarding or even torture in the future, and they look back into history for the position of the church when such techniques were used during the wars against terrorism at the beginning of the twenty-first century, they may decide to employ such techniques under the belief that they are scripturally and theologically sound.

What is really at stake is whether the evangelical church will be a city on a hill. American Presidents from John F. Kennedy to Ronald Reagan have invoked the city on a hill as an example of what America should be. This parable of Jesus[30] first came to America in a sermon

[27] "Ted Cruz, Donald Trump Advocate Bringing Back Waterboarding," video, 3:48, from the Republican Presidential debate televised by abcnews.com on Feb. 6, 2016, http://abcnews.go.com/Politics/video/ted-cruz-donald-trump-advocate-bringing-back-waterboarding-36764410.

[28] "Trump: Waterboarding not tough enough," video, 1:24, from a campaign speech televised by CNN on June 29, 2016, http://www.cnn.com/videos/politics/2016/06/29/trump-waterboarding-not-tough-enough-sot.cnn.

[29] Jeremy Diamond, "Trump on Torture: 'We have to beat the savages'" *CNN*, March 6, 2016, http://www.cnn.com/2016/03/06/politics/donald-trump-torture/.

[30] Matt. 5:14–16: "You are the light of the world. A city set on a hill cannot be hidden. Nor do people light a lamp and put it under a basket, but on a stand, and it gives light to all in the house. In the same way, let your light shine before others, so that they may see your good works and give glory to

written by Puritan John Winthrop aboard a ship crossing the Atlantic Ocean.[31] In the sermon, Winthrop uses the parable not as an ideal to strive for but as a warning to the church that their witness for Christ was at stake. As they sailed to establish the Massachusetts Bay Colony, Winthrop warned them that "the eyes of all people are upon us" to see if their new community will be one that does justly, loves mercy, and walks humbly with their God.[32] Will they be a community of brotherly affection, meekness, gentleness, patience and liberality?[33] If so, then Winthrop believed that God would "dwell among us, as his [own] people, and will command a blessing upon us in all our ways."[34] If they failed, then Winthrop expected that they would cause the mouths of God's enemies to speak evil of God's ways and his people.[35] They would "shame the faces of many of God's worthy servants."[36] And Winthrop believed that God would withdraw his help from them, causing their community to become a by-word for the world.[37]

Wayne Grudem believes that being on the "high moral ground" of "world opinion" is not a worthy desire if the U.S. is viewed as "pampering captured terrorists."[38] Grudem believes that the enemies of the United States do not respect "timidity and weakness, but courage and superior strength." This book argues that inflicting "significant pain"[39] on detainees is not a sign of courage. There is no courage in taking a shackled, defenseless prisoner and slapping him,[40]

---

your Father who is in heaven."

[31] John Winthrop, "A Modell of Christian Charity," The Winthrop Society (1630), http://winthropsociety.com/ doc_charity.php.

[32] Ibid.

[33] Ibid.

[34] Ibid.

[35] Ibid.

[36] Ibid.

[37] Ibid.

[38] Grudem, *Politics According to the Bible*, 429.

[39] Ibid., 430.

[40] Steven G. Bradbury, Memo "Application of United States Obligations Under Article 16 of the Convention Against Torture to Certain Techniques

knocking him into a wall,[41] or convincing him that severely painful consequences and death are imminent for him and his family if he does not answer the interrogator's questions.[42] People show courage on the battlefield—not in the interrogation room. People show courage through actions that exhibit self-sacrifice for the good of others not in the sacrifice of others for the good of self. It is startling to compare what Grudem values about today's America to those values Winthrop hoped for in a nascent America. Winthrop's sermon expresses fears about how Christians in America will act before the eyes of God while Grudem's discussion of interrogation fears how Americans will be perceived before the eyes of their enemies.

Unlike Winthrop, many evangelicals fail to appreciate that their witness for Christ is at stake in their support for detainee abuse. Many Americans believe that the evangelical characterization of terrorists as an "exception"[43] to the prohibition on torture or abuse is a utilitarian rationale that is inconsistent with evangelical positions on abortion, which tend to be deontological. Many Americans have charged that this exception is one of convenience seeking either security or seeking to defend the position of the evangelical president's use of enhanced interrogation techniques. Chuck Colson fell prey to such charges in 2007.

Chuck Colson, founder of Prison Fellowship Ministries, was participating on a panel of religious leaders discussing torture when he wrote that there is an exception to the Christian understanding of human dignity for torture that "might save the lives of thousands."[44]

---

that May Be Used in the Interrogation of High Value al Qaeda Detainees" (May 30, 2005): 7, http://nsarchive.gwu.edu/torture_archive/docs/Bradbury%20memo.pdf.

[41] Ibid.

[42] Major General Michael Dunlavey, "Counter-Resistance Strategies" (Oct. 11, 2002), http://nsarchive.gwu.edu/ torturing democracy/documents/20021011.pdf.

[43] Grudem, *Politics According to the Bible*, 427–28.

[44] Colson, "Justified Under Some Circumstances."

Colson, the man who popularized the concept of having a biblical worldview with his 2004 book *How Now Shall We Live*, cited no Scripture but invoked the Greek philosophical concept of prudence, referenced the words of Dr. Martin Luther King, and compared the torture of prisoners to a person trespassing to rescue a drowning person.[45] Colson's comments produced an immediate response on the internet that lasted for years.[46] One commenter on the *Washington Post's* website wrote, "Chuck, I see not much has changed from the Watergate days when protecting the president required moral relativism."[47] The point of most critics was that evangelicals, who tend to be deontological, created an exception for political reasons and not Scriptural reasons.

This book concludes by hoping that evangelicals will wrestle with Scripture and strive to be that city on a hill. This book hopes that national leaders will follow the example of King Hezekiah instead of King Ahaz. King Hezekiah prepared for war and then trusted in the Lord to deliver him and his people. God honored Hezekiah's faithfulness and delivered his people. King Hezekiah offers a model of faithful leadership for Christian leaders to follow. Christian leaders should seek God's counsel by wrestling with his word and then trusting him to bless their righteous warfare.

[45] Ibid.

[46] John Blake discussed Colson's comments in his article on CNN. John Blake, "Torturing prompts soul-searching among Christians," *CNN*, May 22, 2009, http://www.cnn.com/2009/US/05/22/torture.christian/.

[47] Colson, "Justified Under Some Circumstances."

Bibliography

Augustine. *Confessions*. New York: Barnes & Noble Classics, 2007.

Barrett, C. K. *A Commentary on the Espistle to the Romans*. London: A & C Black, 1991.

Bavinck, Herman. *Reformed Dogmatics*. Edited by John Bolt. Translated by John Vriend. Vol. II. Grand Rapids: Baker Academic, 2004.

Berkhof, Louis. *Systematic Theology*. Grand Rapids: William B. Eerdmans Publishing Company, 1996.

Berkouwer, G. C. *Man: The Image of God*. Grand Rapids: Wm. B. Eerdmans Publishing Company, 1962.

Blake, John. "Torturing prompts soul-searching among some Christians." *CNN*. May 22, 2009. http://www.cnn.com/2009/US/05/22/torture.christian/.

Blumenfeld, Laura. "The Sole Survivor." *Washington Post*, June 11, 2007, A1.

Bonhoeffer, Dietrich. *Ethics*. Translated by Neville Horton Smith. New York: Simon & Schuster, 1995.

Boothby, William H. *The Law of Targeting*. Oxford: Oxford University Press, 2012.

Bradbury, Steven G. "Application of United States Obligations Under Article 16 of the Convention Against Torture to Certain Techniques that May be Used in the Interrogation of High Value al Qaeda Detainees," May 30, 2005. http://nsarchive.gwu.edu/torture_archive/docs/ Bradbury%20memo.pdf.

Branigin, William. "Man Charged with Plotting Shoe Bomb Attack." *Washington Post*, Oct. 4, 2004. http://www.washingtonpost.com/wp-dyn/articles/A6218-2004Oct4.html.

Bravin, Jess. "The Conscience of the Colonel" *Wall Street Journal*, Mar. 31, 2007.

——. *Terror Courts*. New Haven: Yale University Press, 2013.

Bush, George W. "Humane Treatment of Taliban and al Qaeda Detainees," Feb. 7, 2002. http://nsarchive.gwu.edu/NSAEBB/NSAEBB127/02.02.07.pdf.

Bybee, Jay S. "Interrogation of al Qaeda Operative," Aug. 1, 2002. http://nsarchive.gwu.edu/ torturingdemocracy/ documents/20020122.pdf

——. "Memo on Standards of Conduct for Interrogation under 18 U.S.C. §§ 2340–2340A (Aug 1, 2002) ." Aug. 1, 2002.

Calvin, John. *Commentaries on the First Book of Moses Called Genesis*. Vol. 1. Grand Rapids: Baker Books, 2005.

——. *Commentary Upon the Book of Psalms*. Grand Rapids: Baker Books, 2005.

——. *Commentary on a Harmony of the Evangelists*. Vol. 3. Grand Rapids: Baker Books, 2005.

——. *Institutes of the Christian Religion*. Translated by Henry Beveridge. Grand Rapids: Wm. B. Eerdmans, 1989.

Charles, J. Daryl. *Between Pacifism and Jihad: Just War and Christian Tradition*. Downer's Grove, Illinois: InterVarsity Press, 2005.

Clausewitz, Carl von. *On War*. Translated by J. J. Graham. London: Kegan, Trench, Trubner & Co., 1908.

Cole, Darrell. "Darrell Cole on Torture." *First Things* (Jan. 6, 2010). http://www.firstthings.com/blogs/first thoughts/2010/01/darrell-cole-on-torture.

——. "Torture and Just War." *Journal of Religious Ethics* 40, 1 (2012): 26–51.

Colson, Charles. "Justified Under Some Circumstances." *Faith Street*, Nov. 9, 2007. http://www.faithstreet.com/onfaith/2007/11/09/justified-under-some-circumsta/2968.

Corey, David D. and J. Daryl Charles. *The Just War Tradition*. Wilmington, Deleware: Intercollegiate Studies Institute, 2012.

Couch, Stuart. Interview. *Torturing Democracy*. National Security Archive/Washington Media Associates. October 9, 2007, http://nsarchive.gwu.edu/torturingdemocracy/interviews/ stu-art_couch.html.

Cranfield, C. E. B. *Romans*. Grand Rapids: William B. Eerdmans Publishing Company, 1985.

Danner, Mark. "Abu Ghraib: The Hidden Story." *New York Review of Books*. Oct. 7, 2004, http://www.nybooks.com/articles/2004/10/07/abu-ghraib-the-hidden-story/.

Davis, John Jefferson. *Evangelical Ethics*. Phillipsburg, New Jersey: P&R Publishing, 2004.

——. "John Jefferson Davis on Torture." *First Things*. Dec. 10, 2010. http://www.firstthings.com/blogs/firstthoughts/2010/01/john-jefferson-davis-on-torture.

Demy, Timothy J. and J. Daryl Charles. *War, Peace, and Christianity: Questions and Answers from a Just War Perspective*. Wheaton: Crossway, 2010.

Deputy Secretary of Defense. "The Department of Defense Detainee Program." Washington, DC: Department of Defense, 2006.

Diamond, Jeremy. "Trump on Torture: 'We have to beat the savages.'" *CNN*. March 6, 2016, http://www.cnn.com/2016/03/06/politics/donald-trump-torture/.

DiMeglio, Richard P. "The Evolution of the Just War Tradition: Defining *Jus Post Bellum*." *Military Law Review* 186 (2006): 116–63.

Douma, J. *The Ten Commandments*. Translated by Nelson D. Kloosterman. Phillipsburg, New Jersey: P&R Publishing Companny, 1996.

Dunlavey, Michael. "Counter-Resistance Strategies," (Oct. 11, 2002). http://nsarchive.gwu. edu/torturingdemocracy/documents/20021011.pdf

Dunn, James D. G. *Romans 9–16*. Vol. 38b. Dallas: Word Books, 1988.

Elshtain, Jean Bethke. "Reflections on the Problem of 'Dirty Hands.'" In *Torture: A Collection*, by Sanford Levinson. Oxford: Oxford University Press, 2004.

Finn, Peter. "Khalid Sheik Mohammed killed U.S. journalist Daniel Pearl, report finds." *Washington Post*. Jan. 20, 2011. http://www.washingtonpost.com/wp-dyn/content/article/2011/ 01/20/AR2011012000057.html.

Fitzmyer, Jospeh A. *Romans*. New York: Doubleday, 1992.

Frame, John M. *Systematic Theology*. Phillipsburg, New Jersey: P&R Publishing, 2013.

France, R. T. *The Gospel of Matthew*. Grand Rapids: William B. Eerdmans Publishing Company, 2007.

Couch, Stuart. Interview. *Torturing Democracy*. National Security Archive (October 9, 2007), http://nsarchive.gwu.edu/torturingdemocracy/interviews/stuart_couch.html.

Greenberg, Karen and Joshua L. Dratel, ed. *The Torture Papers: The Road to Abu Ghraib*. New York: Caimbridge University Press, 2005.

Grenz, Stanley J. *The Social God and the Relational Self*. Louisville: Westminster John Knox Press, 2001.

Grotius, Hugo. *Law of War and Peace*. Vol. 2. Translated by A. C. Campbell. Kitchener, ON: Batoche Books, 2001. http://socserv2.socsci.mcmaster.ca/econ/ugcm/3ll3/grotius/Law2.pdf.

Grudem, Wayne. *Politics According to the Bible*. Grand Rapids: Zondervan, 2010.

——. *Systematic Theology*. Grand Rapids: Zondervan, 2000.

Hagner, Donald A. *Matthew 14–28*. Dallas: Word Books, 1995.

Hartle, Anthony E. *Moral Issues in Military Decisions Making*. Lawrence, Kansas: University Press of Kansas, 2004.

Haugen, Gary A. "Silence on Suffering." *Christianity Today* (Oct. 17, 2005). http://www.christianitytoday.com/ct/2005/octoberweb-only/12.0b.html.

Headquarters, Department of the Army. *Field Manual 2-22.3 Human Intelligence Collector Operations*. Washington, DC: U.S. Army, Sept. 2006.

——. *Field Manual 34–52 Intelligence Interrogation*. Washington, D.C.: U.S. Army, Sept. 1992.

Heimbach, Daniel R. "Daniel Heimbach on Torture." *First Things* (Jan. 6, 2010). http://www.firstthings.com/blogs/firstthoughts/2010/01/daniel-heimbach-on-torture.

——. "The Problem with Assessing Torture." http://www.phc.edu/UserFiles/File/_Other%20Projects/Global%20Journal/10-1/Daniel_Heimbach_Torture_vol_10_no_1.pdf.

Henry, Matthew. *Isaiah to Malachi*. Vol. 4, in *Commentary on the Whole Bible*. Hendrickson Publishers, 1998.

Hersh, Seymour. "The General's Report." *New Yorker*, Jun 25, 2007. http://www.newyorker.com/magazine/2007/06/25/the-generals-report.

Higham, Scott and Joe Stephens. "New Details of Prisoner Abuse Emerge." *Washington Post*, May 21, 2004, https://www.washingtonpost.com/archive/politics/2004/05/21/new-details-of-prison-abuse-emerge/7346e4cb-47f8-42ab-8897-38a021a1bd0c/.

Hill, James T. "Counter-Resistance Techniques," (Oct. 25, 2002). http://nsarchive.gwu.edu/ torturingdemocracy/documents/20021025.pdf.

Himes, Kenneth R. "The United States at War: Taking Stock." *Theological Studies* 71 (2010): 190–209.

Hoekema, Anthony A. *Created in God's Image*. Grand Rapids: Wm. B. Eerdmans Publishing Company, 1986.

Horton, Michael. *The Christian Fatih: A Systematic Theology*. Grand Rapids: Zondervan, 2011.

How, William Walsham. "For All the Saints." *Trinity Hymnal*. Atlanta, GA: Great Commission Publishing, 1990.

Independent Panel to Review DoD Detention Operations. *Final Report*. August 2004. http://nsarchive.gwu.edu/torturingdemocracy/documents/20040824.pdf.

International and Operational Law Department. *The Law of War Deskbook*. Charlottesville, Virginia: U.S. Army Judge Advocate General's Legal Center and School, 2004.

International Committee of the Red Cross. "Report of the International Committee of the Red Cross (ICRC) on the Treatment of Prisoners of War by Coalition Personnel and other Protected Persons by the Geneva Conventions in Iraq during Arrest, Internment, and Interrogation." In *The Torture Papers*. Edited by Karen Greenberg and Joshua Dratel. Caimbridge: Caimbridge University Press 2006.

Jeffreys, Derek S. *Spirituality and the Ethics of Torture*. New York: Palgrave Macmillan, 2009.

Jenson, Robert W. *Systematic Theology*. Vol. 2. New York: Oxford, 1999.

Jewett, Robert. *Romans: A Commentary*. Minneapolis: Fortress Press, 2009.

Johnson, James Turner. *Can Modern War Be Just?* New Haven: Yale University Press, 1984.

——. *Ideology, Reason, and the Limitation of War*. Princeton, New Jersey: Princeton University Press, 1999.

——. E-mail to the Author, Oct. 14, 2014.

——. *Morality and Contemporary Warfare*. New Haven: Yale University Press, 1999.

Johnson, James Turner. "The Broken Tradition." *National Interest* 45 (Fall 1996): 27–36.

——. "Torture: A Just War Perspective." *The Review of Faith & International Affairs* 5, 2 (2007): 29–31.

Kidner, Derek. *Proverbs*. Downers Grove, IL: InterVarsity Press, 2008.

Krauthammer, Charles. "The Truth About Torture: Its Time to be honest about doing terrible things." *Weekly Standard*. Dec. 5, 2005. http://www.weeklystandard.com/the-truth-about-torture/article/7589.

Lauritzen. *The Ethics of Interrogation*. Washington: Georgetown University Press, 2013.

Luban, David. "Liberalism, Torture, and the Ticking Time Bomb." *Virginia Law Review*. 94. 2005: 1425–60.

Markon, Jerry and Spencer S. Hsu. "Probe in failed Times Square attack focusing on Pakistani Taliban." *Washington Post*, May 5, 2010.

Mayer, Jane. *The Dark Side*. New York: Doubleday, 2008.

Meyer, Josh and Peter Nicholas. "Obama calls jet incident a 'serious reminder.'" *Los Angeles Times*, Dec. 29, 2009. http://articles.latimes.com/2009/dec/29/nation/la-na-plane-terror29-2009dec29.

Mohler, R. Albert. "Albert Mohler on Torture." *First Things* (Jan. 6, 2010). http://www. firstthings.com/blogs/firstthoughts/2010/01/albert-mohler-on-torture.

Mora, Alberto. "William V. O'Brien Lecture in International Law and Morality at Georgetown University," Washington, D.C., Apr. 30, 2013.

Mouw, Richard. "Original Sin in Abu Ghraib." *Beliefnet*, July 23, 2009. http://www.beliefnet.com/Faiths/Christianity/2004/05/Original-Sin-In-Abu-Ghraib.aspx?p=2.

Murray, John. *Principles of Conduct: Aspects of Biblical Ethics*. Grand Rapids: Wm. B. Eerdmans Publishing, 1957.

———. *The Epistle to the Romans*. Vol. 2. Grand Rapids: Wm. B. Eerdmans Publishing, 1965.

Obama, Barak. *Barak Obama, Executive Order 13491 Ensuring Lawful Interrogations*. Jan. 22, 2009.

O'Brien, William Vincent. *The Conduct of Just and Limited War*. New York: Praeger Publishers, 1981.

Orend, Brian. *The Morality of Warfare*. Toronto: Broadview Press, 2006.

Patterson, Eric. *Just War Thinking: Morality and Pragmatism in the Struggle agaisnt Contemporary Threats*. Lanham, MD: Lexongton Books, 2007.

Pavlischek, Keith. "Reinhold Niebuhr, Christian Realism, and Just War Theory: A Critique." In *Christianity and Power Politics Today*, by Eric Patterson. New York: Palgrave Macmillan, 2008.

Pew Research. "The Religious Dimensions of the Torture Debate." *Religion & Public Life Project*, Apr. 29, 2009. http://www.pewforum.org/2009/04/29/the-religious-dimensions-of-the-torture-debate/.

———. "The Torture Debate: A Closer Look." *Religion & Public Life Project*, May 7, 2009.

Phifer, Jerald. "Request for Approval of Counter-Resistance Strategies" (Oct. 11, 2002). http://nsarchive.gwu.edu/torturingdemocracy/documents/20021025.pdf.

Priest, Dana and Barton Gellman. "U.S. Decries Abuse but Defends Interrogations." *Washington Post*, Dec. 26, 2002.

Ramsey, Paul. *Basic Christian Ethics*. Louisville, Kentucky: Westminster John Knox Press, 1950.

——. *The Just War: Force and Political Responsibility*. Lanham, Maryland: Rowman & Littlefield Publishers, Inc., 2002.

Redacted Name. *E-Mail from an Army Officer in Fourth Infantry Division*, Aug. 14, 2003: available at http://www.torturingdemocracy.org/documents/20030814.pdf.

Riechmann, Deb. "Bush Declares: 'We Do Not Torture.'" *Washington* Post, November 7, 2005, http://www.washingtonpost.com/wp-yn/content/article/2005/11/07/AR200511070052 1_pf.html.

Rumsfeld, Donald. "Counter Resistance Techniques," (Dec. 2, 2002). http://nsarchive.gwu.edu /torturingdemocracy/documents/20021127-1.pdf.

Rutledge, Fleming. "My Enemy, Myself: A Sermon." In *Torture is a Moral Issue*, edited by George Hunsinger. Grand Rapids: William B. Eerdmans Publishing Company, 2008.

Rutledge, Fleming. "Abu Ghraib and the Mind of the Trinity." June 6, 2003, http://www. generousorthodoxy.org/sermons/abu-ghraib-and-the-mind-of-the-trinity.aspx.

Savage, Charlie. "Election Day to Decide Future Interrogation Methods in Terrorism Cases." *New York Times*, Sept. 27, 2012.

Schmidt, Randall and John Furlow. *Investigation into FBU Allegations of Detainee Abuse at Guantanamo Bay, Cuba Detention Facility*, (June 9, 2005), http://nsarchive.gwu.edu/ torturingdemocracy/documents/20050400.pdf.

Shane, Scott. "Waterboarding used 266 times on 2 suspects." *New York Times*. Apr. 19, 2009. http://www.nytimes.com/2009/04/20/world/20detain.html?_r =0.

Sherlock, Charles. *The Doctrine of Humanity*. Downer's Grove, IL: InterVarsity Press, 1996.

Stated Clerk of the General Assembly of the Presbyterian Church in America. "The Shorter Catechism." In *The Westminster Confession of Faith*. Committee for Christian Education & Publications, 1990.

Taguba, Antonio M. "AR 15-6 INVESTIGATION OF THE 800TH MILITARY POLICE BRIGADE." 2004. http://nsarchive.gwu.edu/NSAEBB/NSAEBB140/TR3.pdf.

"Ted Cruz, Donald Trump Advocate Bringing Back Waterboarding." Video. 3:48. From the Republican Presidential debate televised by abcnews.com on Feb. 6, 2016. http://abcnews.go.com/Politics/video/ted-cruz-donald-trump-advocate-bringing-back-waterboarding-36764410.

"The Heidelberg Catechism." Available at http://www.wts.edu/resources/creeds/heidelberg.html. 1563.

The Holy Bible, English Standard Version. Wheaton, IL: Crossway Bibles, 2000.

Thomas, Cal. "Torturing Ourselves to Death." *Faith Street*, Nov. 13, 2007. http://www.faithstreet.com/onfaith/2007/11/13/torturing-ourselves-to-death/1091.

"Trump: Waterboarding not tough enough." Video. 1:24. From a campaign speech televised by CNN on June 29, 2016. http://www.cnn.com/videos/politics/2016/06/29/trump-waterboarding-not-tough-enough-sot.cnn.

Unknown Interrogator. "Interrogation Log 063." Nov. 23, 2002. http://american torture.com/documents/gitmo/13.pdf.

U.S. Senate Committee on Armed Services. Inquiry into the Treatment of Detainees in U.S. Custody (Nov 20, 2008). http://www.armed-services.senate.gov/imo/media/doc/Detainee-Report-Final_April-22-2009.pdf.

VanGemeron, Willem A. *Interpreting the Prophetic Word.* Grand Rapids: Zondervan, 1990.

Vatican. *Catechism of the Catholic Church.* Vatican: Vatican, 1997.

Wagner, Lindsey. "Former Guantanamo Bay Prosecutor Shares Story." *University of Virginia School of Law* (Feb. 19, 2009). http://www.law.virginia.edu/html/news/2009_spr/ colonel.htm.

Waltke, Bruce K. *The Book of Proverbs: Chapters 1–15.* Grand Rapids: William B. Eerdmans Publishing Company, 2004.

——. *The Book of Proverbs: Chapters 15–31.* Grand Rapids: William B. Eerdmans Publishing Company, 2005.

Walzer, Michael. *Just and Unjust Wars: A Moral Argument with Historical Illustrations.* New York: Perseus Books Group, 2006.

——. "Political Action: the Problem of Dirty Hands." *Philosophy and Public Affairs* 2, 2 (Winter 1973): 160–80.

——. "Political Action: The Problem of Dirty Hands." In *Torture: A Collection*, by Sanford Levinson, 61–75. Oxford: Oxford University Press, 2006.

Warrick, Joby and Dan Eggen, "Waterboarding Recounted." *Washington Post*, December 11, 2007. http://www.washingtonpost.com/wpdyn/content/article/2007/12/10/AR20071210020 91.html.

Washington Post. "God in Government." May 9, 2009.

Weber, Harry R. "Former Olympic Park Guard Jewell Dies." *Washington Post*, Aug 30, 2007, http://www.washingtonpost.com/wp-dyn/content/article/2007/08/30/AR2007083000 324_pf.html.

Wigg-Stevenson, Tyler. "Tortured Truth." In *Religious Faith, Torture, and Our National Soul*, edited by David P. Gushee. Macon, Georgia: Mercer University Press, 2010.

Winthrop, John. *A Modell of Christian Charity.* Boston: Collections of the Massachusetts Historical Society, 1630.

Woodward, Bob. "Detainee Tortured, Says U.S. Official." *Washington Post*, Jan. 14, 2009: A1.

Zernike, Kate. "The Reach of War: The Witnesses; Only a Few Spoke Up on Abuse As Many Soldiers Stayed Quiet." *New York Times*, May 22, 2004. http://www.nytimes.com/2004/05/22/ world/reach-war-witnesses-only-few-spoke-up-abuse-many-soldiers- stayed-silent.html.

Index of Scripture

Index of Subjects and Names

Porter Harlow recently retired as a Lieutenant Colonel in the U.S. Marine Corps, where he served as an operational law attorney. In past assignments, he served as the Staff Judge Advocate for Second Marine Aircraft Wing (Forward) during its deployment to the Al Anbar Province of Iraq. He served as the senior Marine instructor and as an associate professor of international and operational law at the U.S. Army's Judge Advocate General's School in Charlottesville, Virginia. There he taught classes on the law of war, comparative law, and rules of engagement in the school's master of laws program. He also served as the Head of the Operational Law Department for the Department of the Navy's Judge Advocate General. In that assignment, he served on the Department of Defense (DoD) Law of War Working Group during the preparation and publication of the first *Department of Defense Law of War Manual.*

Porter Harlow is a graduate of the Citadel (B.A.), the University of South Carolina's School of Law (J.D.), and the U.S. Army Judge Advocate General's Legal Center and School (LL.M.). While he was stationed at the Pentagon, he graduated from Reformed Theological Seminary, Washington, D.C., with a Master of Arts in Religion (M.A.R.).

Porter Harlow has served as a ruling elder on the session of two churches in the Presbyterian Church in America (PCA), one in the Palmetto Presbytery and the other in the Potomac Presbytery.

Available in the Reformed Academic Dissertation Series

◆

How Should We Treat Detainees? An Examination of "Enhanced Interrogation Techniques" under the Light of Scripture and the Just War Tradition,
by J. Porter Harlow

Marks of Saving Grace: Theological Method and the Doctrine of Assurance in Jonathan Edwards's A Treatise Concerning Religious Affections,
by Eric J. Lehner

Forthcoming

From Inscrutability to Concursus: Benjamin B. Warfield's Theological Construction of Revelation's Mode from 1880 to 1915,
by Jeffrey A. Stivason

It Has Not Yet Appeared What We Shall Be: A Reconsideration of the Imago Dei *in Light of Those with Severe Cognitive Disabilities*,
by George C. Hammond

Preaching with Biblical Motivation: How to Incorporate the Motivation Found in the Inspired Preaching of the Apostles into Your Sermons,
by Ray E. Heiple Jr.

The Triune God of Unity in Diversity: An Analysis of Perspectivalism, the Trinitarian Theological Method of John Frame and Vern Poythress,
by Timothy E. Miller